REAL ESTATE WITH JOY

A Broker's Tales of the Trails that Lead Home

JOY SHULMAN EARLS

SPS
SELF-PUBLISHING SERVICES LLC
HELPING YOU WITH ALL YOUR PUBLISHING NEEDS

Edited by Self Publishing Services
selfpublishingservices@gmail.com

Cover Design by Renata Strauss
Book Layout by Renata Strauss

Acknowledgment

The articles included in Real Estate with Joy were originally published in the Missoulian. They are included here with the newspaper's permission. They are similar in content, but have been edited to fit a book format.

To Mark

Thanks for sitting at your desk next
to mine in our home office,
in silence, waiting for the inevitable alarmed cry:
"Can you look this over?
My deadline is tomorrow at noon."

Table of Contents

Forward _____ *iv*

CHAPTER 1

Downsizing, Rightsizing?—My First Story _____ 2

Easy Tip To Help You Remember Chores—
Save Time for the Fun Things in Life _____ 6

Moving?—Should You Buy or Rent? _____ 9

'I'm Going To Live Here Forever'—
Planning for the Opposite _____ 12

Consider Your Pets When Buying or Selling a Home _____ 15

CHAPTER 2

Trust your Taste _____ 20

Repair or Replace?—How to Decide? _____ 23

CHAPTER 3

Storage Wars?—
Don't Be Embarrassed When You Open That Door _____ 28

Throw It or Keep It?—Treasures vs. Garbage? _____ 31

CHAPTER 4

Buying or Selling?—"thinkidover" _____ 36

Stay Focused—Don't Get Hung Up on Irrelevant Things _____ 40

Pitfalls of Buying and Selling—Be Cautious _____ 43

Hidden Costs When Buying or Selling—
'Not the Rabbit Ears!' _____ 47

CHAPTER 5

Gather a Team—
Seek Professionals Who Know Their Business _____ 52

Hone Your Math Skills—Know Your Costs _____ 56

A Real Estate Quiz _____ 59

First-Time Buyers—Put a Process in Place _____ 64

CHAPTER 6

Getting Your Home Ready for Sale—Staging and Photos _____ 70

Be Cautious When Showing Your Home—
Don't Get Sidetracked by a Thief _____ 73

Personal Property vs. Real Property—
What Are You Selling? _____77

Inspections—Important for Both Buyers and Sellers _____ 81

CHAPTER 7

The Perfect Mother's Day Gifts _____ 86

A True Story About a Mom and Her Family—
Think About the Reality _____ 90

Live With a Support System in Place—
Independently at Home _____ 94

Cooperative Living—An Attractive Option _____ 97

Cohousing—Another Unique Living Opportunity_____ 101

Afterward_____ 104

About the Author _____ 106

Forward

Real estate has been a force in my life, both intentionally and sub-liminally, since I helped my father, George Shulman, do his chores around the house in the 1960s. He was a proud homeowner, having built his home as so many other Americans did in the boom after World War II. As a son of immigrants raised during the Depression, he taught me to be self-suffi-cient. I helped him change the element in our electric range more than once. I watched him mix concrete to repair our back steps. He taught me about those steel I-beams in the garage that supported my sister Shelley's bedroom above.

After his passing in 1999, memories flooded back as I cleared the house, preparing it for sale. Although he hadn't been in the basement for years, I was drawn to the wooden shelves he had built along one wall. They were opposite the ping-pong table and behind a clothesline my mother used in winter because we didn't have a dryer. Everything he needed for home re-pairs was there. Glass jars filled with screws and nails sat next to a hammer and screwdrivers, hand trowels, hand saws, and a hand drill. There were no power tools in our home.

I wanted to hear, just one more time, "Joy, can you bring me up a Phillips? That's the one with the funny tip." Of course, he knew that I knew that. Then, through a tearful eye with a small smile, I realize why I often tell my boys, Carter and Leland, the same stories, even when they've heard them many times before.

This compilation of real estate stories is winnowed from articles I wrote for the *Missoulian*. I got the idea when I was working as a real estate broker. I started seeing patterns in conversations, debates, discussions, and questions when meeting with clients or talking with others in our profession. At the time, it seemed easier to write one article about a topic and make my point.

That is when I called Sherry Devlin at the *Missoulian* and made my pitch. I am eternally grateful to her for taking the chance, as we had never met, and she also had never read anything I'd written. After the first article was published, I was, to my surprise, asked to write another. Soon thereafter, it wasn't unusual to find in my inbox on a Tuesday an email with a subject line that said, "Deadline Thursday." That was when I realized I was a regular, and as I frantically looked around my desk for clues of what to write about, I could also ask if Friday at 1 p.m. would work.

I gained an enormous respect for journalists and their significant others. Mark, my husband, cringed on Thursdays as I mumbled in front of my computer. He knew he would be pushed into editorial duties as I loudly proclaimed that I could never do this and what was I thinking to come up with such an idea. It is because of his subtle guidance that I started including my (our) personal stories. The first articles were very technical and full of real estate jargon. He suggested that by telling some of our experiences, I could get the point across in a more satisfying way.

The first time I went into the bank and someone stopped me to say his wife cut my article out of the paper for them to keep, I was surprised. I do believe my face went pink. I took care of my business and rushed out to my car. Mark was right.

Over the years, I cut out some of my articles and stuffed them in a manila folder. When a discussion came up about a topic like negotiating a real estate contract, I took out "Not The Rabbit Ears." Or when I was helping people right-size their homes, I took out another.

To make life easier, I took out the manila envelope and compiled them into this book, *Real Estate with Joy.* I still get a chuckle, and sometimes a few tears, when I read some of these.

CHAPTER 1

'I'm going to live here forever...
maybe'

Downsizing, Rightsizing?—My First Story

Downsizing and rightsizing are terms I have written about in articles. The concept isn't terribly difficult to write about, to read about or to think about. Boomers' housing needs are starting to change, along with their lives.

But this week, for me, the concept became a reality. While in the past I have worked with clients and helped others with this difficult task, I now will forever understand it in a more intimate way.

Camping is part of my life. My first experience was at summer camp when I was 10. I was immediately smitten. As an adult, I was captured by backpacking, and any moment I could steal away into the wilderness was a treat.

When our first son, Leland, was born on June 1, at the beginning of the summer, he had to become a part of this love. Then our younger son, Carter, joined us five years later. We found it was taking longer to escape for weekends in the woods, especially with little ones, diapers and naps. And then there were our dogs, who could not be left behind.

A camper made perfect sense. In one place, we could store blankets and toys and a stove to warm milk. We bought one that fit our family perfectly. When days off work arrived, the four of us jumped into the car, hooked up our fun little home on wheels and took off for great adventures. We always started the season at Yellowstone National Park on Memorial Day weekend with our dear friends Kathy and Richard and their two boys, Conor and Christian.

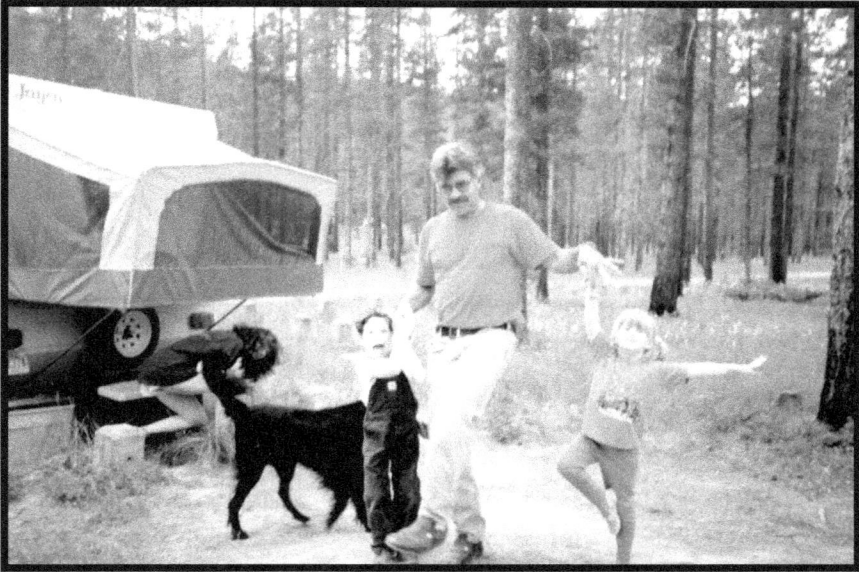

We're setting up our camper, our home away from home. It gave our family infinite fun and infinite stories about that fun.

One year, on a snowy/rainy outing, Kathy surprised me with a deck of cards, picturing Old Faithful on the front. We piled in the camper, drank hot chocolate, played cards and laughed about buffalo poop in the campground. When claustrophobia kicked in, the boys ran out and whittled by the campfire. After they went off for a hike, I sneaked down, picked up their artwork and hid the wood sculptures in the back of a drawer.

One by one, new relics became a part of this home on wheels. I found the perfect teapot. We splurged and bought a popcorn maker for the campfire. Soon, each nook held our special belongings. Fishing poles were ready to grab at a moment's notice, the firewood saw was handy when needed, a special pan for frying trout waited for our catch, and my bird book was always necessary because my husband calls every bird a canary.

Carter could never nap because he didn't want to miss out on the adventures outside.

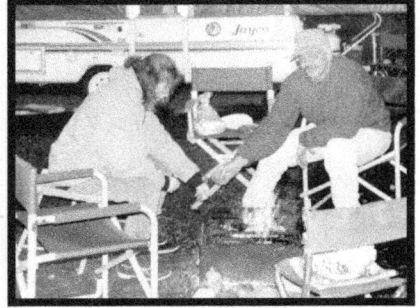

Everything always tastes better when you're in the woods.

I never knew a little camper could carry such a cache, and all of it just for pure fun.

My sister Shelley visited from Boston one summer, and we took her along on one of our camping outings to the Big Hole Valley. It was cold and raining, and we were cooking steaks over the fire under a tarp. We pulled down the table in the kitchen, piled on a down blanket and she snuggled in for the night. She, too, was smitten.

The years rolled by, and as the boys grew older, other commitments postponed some of the weekends with our camper. Soon Kathy and I would start talking in January so we could be sure that whatever came up, we wouldn't miss our Memorial Day in Yellowstone. I can't remember the first time we missed, but I think it was a graduation. OK, that was important enough. We couldn't miss a child's graduation! This year our younger son, Carter, will be the last of the boys to graduate from high school. Last year, Leland, our elder son, backpacked the entire Pacific Crest Trail. His brother joined him for the John Muir portion, and we all met for some glorious days along that trail.

Carter savors his toasted treat
on a custom-made stick whittled
around the fire and saved in
the camper for next time.

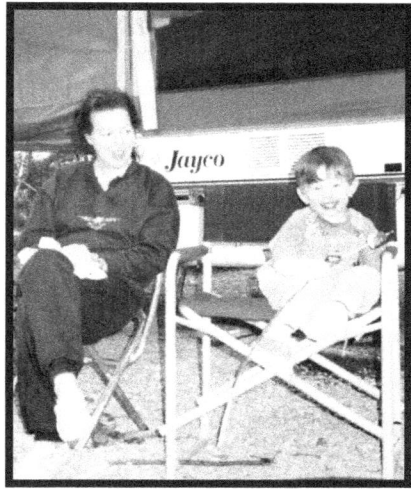

Aunt Shelley from Boston said,
"You never told me camping
was this wonderful!"

Our little camper was parked in the backyard while we were all away. This spring, as I looked out the kitchen window, I knew that we had entered a new phase of our lives. We just don't need a camper that big anymore. The next sunny day, Mark and I opened the camper and started unloading it one last time. I pulled out the silverware, and in the back of the drawer, I found the whittled sticks. Under the sink was a very used deck of cards carefully placed in a plastic case. A task that could have been accomplished in a couple of hours took an entire weekend. Unloading each piece was a memory.

I placed the ad to sell our little camper on Craigslist and received a call immediately. When a young couple (the future owners) arrived to look at our camper, they had their baby boy, Conor, with them. I asked them when he was born and his mom, Kelly, smiled and said his birthday was coming up—June 1, just at the beginning of the summer.

Easy Tip To Help You Remember Chores— Save Time for the Fun Things in Life

When spring is in the air, birds pair up and nest in our town. Some head north to summer grounds, and others are home when they finally reach Missoula. There is a fresh smell in the air. It reminds me that it's time to open the windows and freshen up the house.

If you have decided to sell your home or even if you are just preparing for company, you might be panicking. You struggle with the reality of the work to be done inside when warm, sunny days beckon you outside. I have some ways to trick myself into making these chores easier. Some I learned from friends and family. And others I stumbled onto myself and was pretty pleased with the results.

More than a decade ago, I met my siblings for a rendezvous. Since our parents are gone, we make an effort to reconnect regularly. Las Vegas was the agreed-upon destination because of its easy access and low cost. I was exhausted by day one with little sleep and lots of talk, as we all caught up with one another. At home in Missoula, I love my Sleepytime tea at the end of a long day but didn't even attempt to buy it in Sin City.

As I was unpacking late that first night, I reached into one of the pockets of my suitcase, and there were two sandwich bags. One contained some ground coffee and the other, two Sleepytime tea bags. My sister was in the room, and I remember saying, "Someone is taking care of me!" and she replied, "I wish someone was doing that for me!" It was a complete accident as I am sure I hadn't unpacked thoroughly from my previous trip, which was who knows when.

Now, whenever I return from a trip, I replenish that bag with tea and put it right back into the suitcase. That way, it is there for the next trip. I enjoy it every time and feel like someone is really taking care of me, even if it is me.

I find one of the great parts of growing older is the recurring themes in my life, like spring cleaning, traveling, skiing and camping. After years of practice, the trips, the chores, and the hobbies have become naturally ingrained into my life, and thus, they are more relaxing. And I have more fun and adventure, even if chores are involved.

Mark and I were married for many years before our boys joined our team. We always looked forward to camping, skiing, hiking and road trip adventures. The four of us made it even more fun, but it took a bit more energy and planning to make trips happen. Having a little one in diapers was not going to stop us from trying to take off after work on a Friday afternoon.

When we camped, I made up a list of what we needed each time. One time I put the list in the top of the cook kit and revised it for the next trip. Over the years, that same list became tattered and revised. Diapers were replaced with playing cards and fishing lures. I use the same list today with a few more changes since it's just the two of us more often. Diapers are still off the list for a while longer, I hope.

Now, if I want to run up and ski, a tattered list is handy. I think I know it by heart, but it's fun to quiz myself. I also like to see what is added, like the Advil, and what is deleted, like the candy bars.

Chores are just the same. Someone shared his secret with me a while ago. On the first day of each season, he has a list of reminders. You can't forget it's the first day of spring, summer or fall. So it makes it easy to know there is already a list of some things to get done around the house proactively. Our list includes checking batteries in the smoke detectors, flashlights and other essentials. Furnaces, septic systems and coffeepots need filters cleaned.

I recently learned that it is important to turn off and on water valves under sinks, toilets, and wherever they are installed. My neighbor Michelle recently told me of a big mess she had that could have been prevented if she had known that tip. Apparently, if the valves aren't used, over time they become difficult to close when you need to close them.

In her case, the sink valve was in an area of the home they didn't use much, and a slow leak gave way to a full-blown flood, which ruined the floor. The valves were hopelessly stuck. This is how I learned to turn water valves on and off seasonally. By writing this now, I am reminding myself to do it, and I just added it to my list.

The seasons, spring especially, are a reminder that being proactive makes life easier and more enjoyable. If trees didn't prepare in the fall, spring would not be the same. If you don't have tattered lists lying around the house, like I do, start right now. Grab four pieces of paper and label them spring, summer, fall and winter. Write "change the batteries" and "rotate the water valves" on each page and then put them aside. You'll feel a little better already.

Then hide a little treat in your suitcase, and I guarantee whomever you are traveling with next will be jealous when you pull it out. Just let them know that someone is looking out for you.

Moving? — Should You Buy or Rent?

Moving can be a stressful thought, even for the most adventurous spirits. Changing homes across town, across the state or across the country might bring some people to their knees. A different town may become necessary because of work, health reasons, retirement or family. It may not be a necessity, but a choice to be in another part of the world after many years in one spot. Whether you are a willing participant or are being dragged along, there are some important decisions to make. Should you sell your home and buy a new one? Should you rent for a while and see how the new surroundings look? Should you stay with your grown children and help around their house while getting established? Or maybe you want to just call the whole idea off for another time, which may not come.

Recently I was working for a week in another city. Since I had some free time during the day, I decided to pretend that I was considering moving to this area. Even though I was still in a Montana town and had been there before, thinking about actually living there brought up different thoughts. I was working with an associate from the local area, and he pointed out a walking trail around a popular neighborhood. It was a perfect segue to learning about the pulse of this area. As I walked, I noticed backyards and parked cars. I couldn't help but see whether people shoveled their walks and/or smiled when I passed by. Not one dog ran out and barked at me, which I truly appreciated. I only saw one "Home For Sale" sign and grabbed the flyer from the box. Before I looked at it, I played my usual game to see if I could guess what this home might be listed for. My estimate was high, which would have made me happy if I were really going to move to this area. Quickly I realized I was basing my pricing on the Missoula real estate market, which wasn't accurate.

I think it is natural for most people to compare the real estate market in their current town to the one they are visiting. They go to a new area and try to plug in what they already know. That's not a bad place to start but one that you want to move away from fairly quickly. There are reasons prices are different in different markets. For the boomer generation, this may work to our advantage. Suppose you are moving for reasons other than full-time work; in that case, the new community may be less expensive because employment might be even harder to find. Perhaps the area caters more to recreation and that's just what you want. Getting to understand what makes this area tick will be important to you in the long run. At first, you may be allured by the low cost of living, but then you might find out that some of the services you are used to are not there. Low taxes could mean less long-range planning and higher costs later to pay for deferred maintenance. It is hard to know or understand these issues unless you do some homework.

I always recommend reading homeowner association minutes, if you can find them. And it wouldn't hurt to read City Council and County Commission meeting minutes too. You will gain insight into the politics, economics, culture and people in the area. Some of the most colorful characters arrive at public meetings and certainly help define the fabric of a town, whether they are openly applauded or not. Now take a moment to read the minutes from your current neighborhood or town. It won't take you long to start nodding and agreeing that these summarize the thoughts and actions that surround your everyday life. These are the springboards for morning coffee klatches in local cafes.

In that town I was visiting, I had several conversations with a server who had worked at the same popular spot for over 20 years. There was a painting in this restaurant of the regulars who used to meet for their morning coffee group. She told me that she would wander back to their big table when times were slow and share in the conversations. I sensed she missed those times.

I asked her if the people sitting at the back of the restaurant that morning were the same group. She gave a sad look and said the guys in the painting had either passed away or were too old to stop in now. While she was talking about missing those old friends, I heard a group laugh come from the back table. I could tell this café had a knack for welcoming folks. Something felt comfortable in a way that I couldn't explain except that I was standing there talking to a complete stranger and grinning from infectious laughter in the room that morning.

It's fun to get the feel of a new town. You are never too old to give it a try. You can even just pretend, as I did when I was in a different town for work. It may inspire you to make a change. If you are considering a move, I would suggest visiting or short-term renting for a while, dropping into local places and reading about the area. Try to understand what makes it tick. There is probably a coffee klatch in the back of a local café somewhere waiting for you right now. You may even find yourself chatting with a server who will introduce you to them in the morning.

'I'm Going To Live Here Forever'—
Planning for the Opposite

I'm going to live here forever. I've heard neighbors, friends, relatives and strangers say this. It is a common theme and feeling. Truthfully, I said it myself when I was comfortably settled in my last home, where I lived for over 15 years. I learned that "forever" can sometimes mean as far as I can see at the time. It is helpful to keep in the back of our minds that things change. We may find ourselves in a situation where we need to move. You can keep this in the back of your mind without being obsessive about it. If or when the time comes when you need to or decide to move, it won't be such a daunting task. Because the worst position you may find yourself in is that you want to move but just can't do it. It has become too difficult. You don't have to let this happen.

Most people like to have a home base, a place to settle. But as time goes by, whether we like it or not, things change in our lives. And darn, it seems to happen faster than we can imagine. Today's priorities can quickly sink to the bottom of our lists or disappear while new ones emerge. Some changes we can control, and others take us by surprise. Through all this, our houses still need care and updating, which can't be ignored. Being proactive about your home's needs will pay off big in the long run as will doing the job right the first time.

I remember talking with two neighbors who were arguing over the placement of a barn. One neighbor woke up one morning to see survey stakes in the ground, which appeared to be four corners of a building that were very close to the property line and her home. She knew this was contrary to the covenants. After confronting her neighbor about this, the corners were moved and building progressed. But during the conversation, the neighbor building the barn said she was never going to move. She promised to be a good custodian and keep the barn clean. It didn't matter where the barn was built as she would always be a good neighbor and the placement of the barn would be a nonissue. Six months after the barn was built, her husband was transferred and they sold their home. Because they had done the job right, they didn't have to worry about explaining to the new owners why the barn was too close to the property line. It might have even delayed the sale. The old neighbors who stayed didn't have to worry about new residents not conforming to the neighborhood standards.

Another time, I remember talking with someone who had built a new home. They thought this was the last home they would ever own. As they were building, they planned for only three bedrooms and put in a septic system accordingly, even though allowing for future expansion wouldn't cost much more. Later when they were selling the home, they realized that the room they had converted in the basement required enlarging the septic system. While the cost was not exorbitant, it still held up the sale of the home and cost more than if they had done it originally.

People often want more room in their home. Sometimes the garage seems like the only choice for expansion, but it can be a poor choice if you are giving up indoor parking and storage. Montanans love their garages, especially during cold, snowy winters. While a den and extra space can seem enticing at the time, when it comes to selling, buyers won't like it. I have seen more than one home languish on the market until the sellers tired of hearing that there was no garage. Buyers wanted the storage for their cars and overflow of bicycles, skis and boxes. As soon as the garage was converted back to its original intended use, the home sold. This is more common than you would imagine.

There are so many stories like these. And so many circumstances that we find ourselves in when doing home projects. We aren't thinking about selling our home at the time, but our decisions can definitely affect a sale if we ever do sell. Here are some suggestions to keep in mind next time you have a choice about which direction to take on an update to your home.

Always find out what the building code requirements are in your area and follow them. Do not cut corners because often you will regret that decision, particularly if you end up selling. If you enjoy doing home maintenance yourself, that's great. But don't do it to save money. Much of the time, it will take you longer, you won't have the necessary tools, and it won't come out as nice or last as long as the professional job. Again, if you end up selling, buyers will see the difference, and you won't get as much for your home in the end. Quality work pays off in the short and the long run.

As I get older, I am more careful to never say never. When I hear people say they are never going to move again, I remember when I said it myself.

Consider Your Pets When Buying or Selling a Home

Our pets are our companions, our source of affection and, for some people, our soul mates. They don't ask much in return compared to what they give us every day. Studies continue to confirm their benefit to our well-being as we age. However, also as we grow older, our own needs are changing while we have a responsibility to be our pets' consistent caretakers. If you are considering a lifestyle change, retirement or perhaps "rightsizing" from your current home, your pets' needs will be an important part of this decision.

If you are a pet owner and animal lover, you know the first part of planning a trip is how to care for your companions. You consider whether they can join you at a pet-friendly hotel or whether you need boarding or in-home care. Our last trip was easier, as our trusted friend Jackie stayed at our home. The list we left still took a whole page that looked something like this:

First thing in the morning, let the dogs out. Remember to put their collars on. When they come inside, give them breakfast and morning pills. Open up the chickens to let them into the pasture. And don't forget to give the fish some food now and then.

Many of us can remember having long discussions with children, spouses or perhaps our own parents many years ago about the challenges and responsibilities of pet ownership. But if you are like me, it is all over once you make the mistake of "just going to look" at a new pet. Our logical, adult reasoning can easily be trumped by a puppy, a kitten or even a guin-

Norman (2008-2021) shared everything with me, including my birthday.

ea pig named Mr. Henry from my son's first-grade class. More than once
—many times more — I found myself headed home with smiling faces in
the car and the sound of a new family member.

Now that our boys are older, the number of pets has decreased. When
my husband and I met 35 years ago, I had a mutt named Jesse, and he had
Sparky. Jesse and Sparky became fast friends, as we did too. Jesse moved to
Missoula with me, and after his passing, I had an oil painting made of him.
Our friendship and time together marked a major passage in my life. Sparky
died of old age while we were camping. We buried her there in the Big Hole
Valley. This is still a favorite place to camp and think of her wonderful spirit.
This was before we had children, when our lives became much busier.

Leland and Sammy, his 'brother.' He was a much better pet than a cricket.

For a short time, we were a pet-free household. Then, as a young boy, our older son Leland came to us with his bug box in hand. He patiently explained to us that he really would love a pet that might interact a little more with him than a cricket.

It was hard to argue, just as it was hard to dispute when Carter, our younger son, noticed that two dogs were happier than just one. I fell for that hook, line and sinker. And I am sure you can picture how we progressed with fish and birds and lizards and chickens and all the other wonderful friends that make up our home.

However, time has passed and Carter is now in college. Leland has long since graduated and is on his own adventures. We are still the pet lovers we have always been. But now we find that our lives are changing. And I think that if you have read this far, you may be in a similar situation. I could never or would never part with our dogs, Norman and Carl, or the fish (never did get a name) or others. And I would encourage you to enjoy each day with them, as the hardest part is that their lives are so short. Losing a pet is impossibly difficult and heartbreaking.

Looking forward to what our next adventures might bring also encourages us to think hard before getting a new pet right away. If you may even be contemplating selling your home in the future and rightsizing, consider your pet responsibilities, too. It is much easier to sell a home that is pet-free. Even all the pet lovers in the world would rather purchase a pet-free home. No one wants to deal with stained carpeting, scratched flooring and odors. In our case, Carl left us a hole in the bedroom wall. What dog chews a hole in Sheetrock?

Also consider where you could be moving or whether you may have a more mobile lifestyle. In either case, caring for a pet may alter your decisions. You might find a home you like, but there may be policies and rules regarding pets, including their sizes and types. I recently learned of a 55-and-older community where only dogs of a certain height at the shoulders are allowed. I didn't understand it at first, because most policies are by weight. However, I noticed dachshunds' weights, for example, can vary from 15 to 40 pounds depending on lifestyle or owner's indulgences.

Rightsizing your home also includes thinking about your pets or perhaps future companions. This may not be the time to replace the dog or cat you recently lost. Enjoy the memories of your irreplaceable companion. Don't try to hold onto the past by finding a young one of the same breed or size. You may want to ask yourself if it's time to start considering the value of a smaller pet. Perhaps you may decide to just return to the simple pleasures of crickets and birds?

CHAPTER 2

'I should do this myself?
It's cheaper—right?'

Trust your Taste

Holiday seasons always seem just around the corner. Festive times are fun in many ways but can quickly turn stressful. Our list of errands gets longer as we prepare the house for more activities than usual. Inviting people into one's home can be uncomfortable. To some, the stress is second only to public speaking. The key to unlocking this door is to have a home that suits you and embodies your lifestyle. And whether you are buying a home, remodeling or even building a new one, remind yourself that it's all about you. Your needs, your style, your interests, your life and what makes you the king or queen of your household should be top of the list. Don't get bogged down by trying to be the person in the glossy pictures of a magazine. Don't choose a home or make your home into something that someone else thinks it should be. Create your own environment around your lifestyle and tastes. It will show, and visitors will feel just as comfortable as you do.

I can think of times in my life and those I know who have stumbled with this notion and even made some costly errors. I doubt my brother would mind if I shared his story. He owns a beautiful stucco home in another part of the country. He and his wife felt their home needed some sprucing up after living there for a decade. They hired a decorator to help choose colors, as they weren't sure what might look good inside and out. When the outside was completed, they realized that they had made a miserable mistake. They would drive up each evening and hurry into the garage, so as not to have to dwell on this mixture of pumpkin and tan and rose. I never saw it; I only heard an anguished description. It was probably the latest color combination but certainly not their taste. They repainted as soon as physically possible, and now, when they pull up to their home, they have a comfortable feeling of being where they belong. My brother says it is one of the costliest mistakes he has made, but worth the expense of changing his house back to a color that made him know he was home. How could he have avoided this whole experience?

Sometimes you just don't know what something will look like or feel like until the changes are done. But the process you use to make decisions that will affect your living arrangement can be carefully thought through. The top priority should be to use your own judgment. If you are unsure, then take the time to think about what you truly like and how a home can complement your particular lifestyle.

Intuitively, you might think that you would know yourself by this time in your life. But as your life changes, your preferences may be different. Decisions can be easy when you are just out of college and get your first job. For many of us, there was only so much money to go around, and decorating was not always the top consideration. I remember when my big transition from college to settling down was to frame the posters that previously had been taped to the wall. The look was much more finished, I thought. As the years went by, and we had a bit more money to spend on sprucing up our home, I thought about what made me feel comfortable. At one time, it was wallpaper. I remember picking out a wall covering that felt just right to me (and I still have it on my walls). My parents' home had some wonderful wallpaper in the kitchen that we all painstakingly hung together.

So as I look back, I guess, for my home, I felt most comfortable reading the paper with a cup of coffee surrounded by warm walls reminiscent of homey mornings. After the paper was hung, a person came in to measure for window blinds. She looked around and said, "I didn't realize people were still doing this," as she pointed to the paper on the walls. Let's say, the tone was not complimentary. Years later, a neighbor came by and told me that she knew someone who would just love our home if we were ever going to sell. "After all, the wallpaper could always be removed."

In a way, she made my point. My kitchen suits **me**. If she ever buys my home, she can change the kitchen to suit **her.**

Repair or Replace? — How to Decide?

Owning a home is a true labor of love. There are always chores and jobs on the "to-do" list. Some of us enjoy puttering around our house, making sure filters are changed, windows are washed and faucets aren't leaking. What has become harder to figure out is whether something that has broken should be fixed or replaced. I am fairly stubborn and optimistic at the same time, so I usually try the former option first. If at all possible, I look for parts to replace or try to reuse a part that isn't totally broken. Is it worth it? Should I just go buy a new item? Should I fix it, or should I call someone to come in and take a look?

I grew up in a sturdy home built in the '50s. My father proudly told the story of visiting with the builder as he was working on our home. The builder was an immigrant who, with his son, built many of the homes in my childhood neighborhood. As I was growing up, I would follow my father around the house as he pointed out certain beams in the garage and stonework painstakingly placed in the front. My father was a chemist and later a mathematician, so the building trades were certainly not his background. I gathered from his walks with me around our house that he respected the craftsmanship and watched the process carefully.

My parents were children of the Great Depression. We reused aluminum foil, which was stored in a kitchen drawer overflowing with rubber bands saved from newspapers. We were possibly the last people I knew to have a refrigerator with an icebox the size of a mailbox. My parents never owned a dryer, so during the winter, our clothes were either in the basement or freeze-drying on the line.

Hanging drywall! One of the many jobs for which you should hire a professional.

On weekends, there were always chores around the house. Even the best-built home, over time, needs repairs. I remember my dad changing the electric element in the oven more than once. I can still see him stirring a cement mixture to repair the back steps. And I can hear his voice calling up from the basement as he checked the fuses to see if the lights came on wherever he told me to stand and watch. He must have been working on something electrical and was seeing if it was working again. I doubt I was much help. But I did rake leaves and shovel snow. And I know now that I was paying more attention to what he was doing than I thought. I honestly don't remember anyone coming in to fix anything in our home except a plumber, after we had lived there for 40 years. My father just couldn't believe that something could be wrong with the plumbing and, even more, that he had to pay someone to fix a problem with *his* home.

When I became a homeowner, this was the only attitude I knew. If something broke, I would try to figure out how to fix it. Luckily, I married someone in the building trades, so I have a convenient person to call when something around the house breaks. But we still have the same questions about when it's time to replace something rather than fix it.

Yesterday we finally decided we were tired of fighting with one of our "stringless blinds" that miraculously pop up and down to open and close. The first time it broke, it was on warranty, so we only had to pay for shipping and handling and wait six months before it was in place again. Just a couple of years later, we found ourselves in the same situation. The blind was hanging at an angle halfway down the window, hopelessly frozen. After climbing on ladders with one of us holding the top and the other maneuvering the bottom, we took it down. We laid it on the dining table, looked inside at the mechanism as one of us held on and tried to move it up or down. We almost had it tackled when the string disappeared into the material. This battle of humans over parts and pieces wasn't over yet. Sadly, the parts were plastic, and the pieces were coming apart. The table was covered with needle-nosed pliers, screwdriver sets, tweezers and a notepad in case one of us thought of a better idea. As tensions rose, my husband was muttering mild profanities about premolded plastic and maniacal mechanisms not made to last. Finally we calmed down, moved a blind that works to the window we use more frequently, and relegated the broken one to the back room. Our conclusion, which is becoming more frequent, is that this item was not made to repair. It is hard for me to accept, which is why I keep trying to repair rather than replace.

I was raised by parents from the Depression era. My father nourished my interests in not only home ownership but also in taking an active role in maintenance. I think he would have a hard time today deciding to replace broken things rather than repair them. I still try to save aluminum foil and hang my clothes on the line. I won't be deliberately wasteful if I

Hire someone who likes their job and does it well!

have options. Frequently I realize that I save time and money by replacing rather than repairing.

Over the years when I visited my dad, I would go through the house and try to fix things, often with my husband on the line giving me directions. Sometimes, when it was just impossible, I arranged repairs when my dad might not notice. My father enjoyed and lived in the same home for the rest of his years without calling in another repairman. The future doesn't look the same for me, but I will keep trying.

CHAPTER 3

(It's all about the stuff)

*Our cherished belongings. Our
treasures. Anchors away!*

Storage Wars?—Don't Be Embarrassed When You Open That Door

I am not an avid reality show viewer; however, I do occasionally get a kick out of *Storage Wars*.

In case you haven't watched it, the crew films the show on location at a variety of storage facilities in California. An auctioneer meets with potential buyers at a facility each week, and the highest bidders win storage units filled with a surprise collection of stuff.

I enjoy the part when they first open the storage door—with music leading up to the clipping of the lock and the first sight of the contents. Buyers are only allowed to look over the contents and not rummage through anything. Most of the time—85 percent?—I think, "What a bunch of junk." Then I wonder how much money the owners of those belongings must have paid to store items that they never retrieved. Is this an American phenomenon? I'm not sure.

I know that before we moved about 10 years ago, the first thing I did was rent a storage unit. I went through belongings, gave some away, threw some away and stored the rest. There were family discussions about what was really necessary to move to the new house and what was borderline. As I look back, I'm sure my husband appeased me by consenting to a storage unit rental.

After moving and settling in, at least one more year went by. We finally agreed on a day when we would make one last trip and decide what to do with the remaining contents of the unit. That morning, we got in

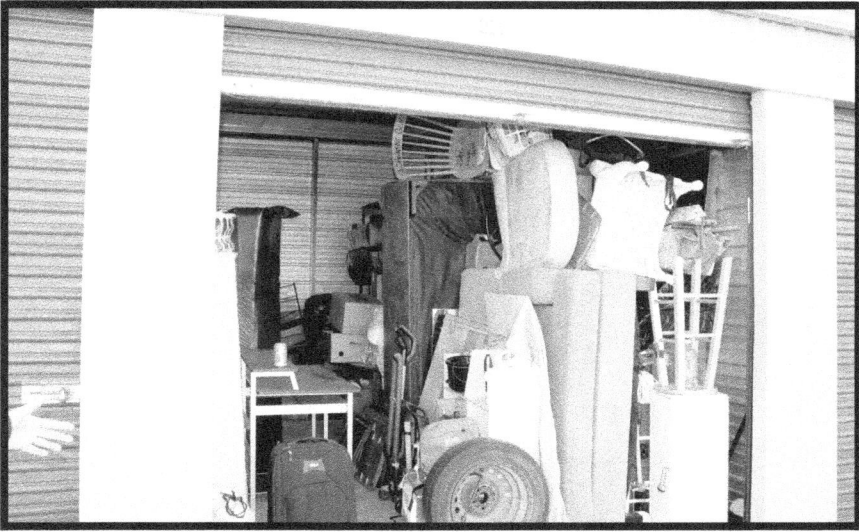

Open that storage unit door, gaze at your treasured belongings, and then load them all up. Next stop, the dump.

the truck, our sons followed in another car and we headed for the storage facility. We estimated it would take two to three truckloads to bring everything home. I was getting excited, as I had forgotten many of our treasures that were packed away.

Just like in *Storage Wars,* my husband popped open the lock and rolled up the door. When we were finished unpacking, we did have three pickup loads, which went directly to the dump. The boys filled the car with the rest and headed home.

This is where my 85 percent estimate comes in. I think, at most, 15 percent of what was in the unit came home with us. How did that happen? These essentials, after moving, became forgotten, and I could barely recall what was so important about them in the first place.

As baby boomers, many of us are considering "rightsizing" our lives. When I work with clients, I often recommend that they get a storage unit immediately. As I look back, I see it as part of a larger process. Are we really storing our important belongings? Or is this a helpful step, psychologically, in making a transition? If you think of it that way, it isn't a very expensive way to move forward.

My sister lives in a large city, where storage units can be a necessity because of space issues. She thought for years that it was imperative to have one. In the same breath, she told me about the time she was hurrying to go on a trip somewhere and needed her suitcase, which of course was in the storage unit. It was quicker and easier for her to buy a new one nearby instead of making arrangements to get to her unit. She ended up liking the new suitcase better and the old one was never used again. But it sat in the locker for many more years.

Besides the obvious cost of paying to store items you can't even remember you have, wouldn't it be better if people who had a more immediate need for those things could use them? I know that is a noble thought and easier said than done.

Here is my advice. Watch *Storage Wars* a few times. Let your mind wander and wonder about the owners of these possessions. Maybe think about what was happening in their lives when they packed those things in there and where the owners might be today. Then rent a locker anyway, so you can move into your new home and move on with your life. It may even be entertaining to reflect about the day when the lock on your unit is popped open and someone—maybe you—peers in and wonders what it cost to store all that obsolete stuff.

Throw It or Keep It?—Treasures vs. Garbage?

How do you know when it's time to throw something away? How do you know when something has passed its point of usefulness? When does a household item that was once so important become just another thing to store or pile up or give away someday — but not today?

When it comes time to sell your home or rightsize or just lighten up your lifestyle, will your material surroundings stop you from moving forward? They do for some people. Even for those who don't have a problem giving away obsolete things, the time-consuming process of sorting through all the stuff can still be a difficult job.

At a local estate sale, where the family was lovely and the people assisting with the sale were working tirelessly, I was exhausted watching people bustling in and out of the home looking for treasures. But I freely admit that I found one myself. I bought a wonderful dining set that I love. My husband wasn't there, but I know our household rule. When one new thing comes into the house, at least one must leave. In this case, the choice was going to be easy, as I definitely don't need two tables and chairs in my kitchen.

While I cleared off our old round oak dining table, Carter, our son, came down. When I told him what was happening, he asked what was wrong with this set. He had eaten meals around this old table for as long as he could remember. We drove it home in our van from Canada on a family vacation. While I thought he seemed sentimental, which I loved, I think he also thought all this work wasn't necessary, as we had a perfectly good kitchen set. And there were so many memories of Thanksgivings and friends and family sharing a meal together. Why do things need to change?

I absorbed that feeling and went right up to our loft over the detached shop, where we store things not used every day. I asked Carter to help me rearrange. We moved an antique desk needing repair to the right and some framed pictures to the left to make room for the old kitchen table and chairs. Then I went back to the house and found all the round tablecloths collected over the years, which I neatly folded and put in a plastic cover. Surely one day, one of our boys will love the round oak table with chairs and use it in their home with this great assortment of covers.

When I put the cloths with the table in the loft, my thoughts returned to that estate sale. There were so many cherished items in their home. I remembered the family sitting on a couch in the living room, tired beyond words. Losing a family member is heart-wrenching enough. Dealing with all the belongings looked overwhelming.

I have helped couples, widows, families and out-of-town estates prepare homes for sale. I remember looking at neatly piled linens, perhaps from beds long gone. And I remember seeing rooms of furniture long past their usefulness. Some of these people must have had the same thoughts I did about my table. They think their children will enjoy them or someday they will be useful. But often families are all over the country or not interested in their parents' things. What was once a cherished item can become another burden.

If at all possible, families should have discussions about family treasures. Everyone should be honest about what could be useful to them someday and what can be given to someone who will use it today. "Antiques Roadshow" has been popular over the years. One reason is that viewers may picture themselves discovering something of worth in their home or loft. But how often does it truly happen that someone doesn't know the approximate value of an item or at least that it is rare or unusual?

Most of our treasures are not worth small fortunes. Instead, for some people, these collections are like anchors, keeping their lives from moving forward. They also pile up unnecessary storage costs. Think first about collecting those cherished items. Keep what is important and enjoy what surrounds you. But at the same time, don't allow your material belongings to take on a life of their own and keep you from moving, selling your home, rightsizing or just simplifying.

Sometimes the best way to decide what you need and what is ready to go out the door is to ask for help. Your family may be the best gauge, but you may also want to engage a professional organizer, move manager or sometimes a "take-charge friend."

Next time you see a garage sale sign, stop and look at what is for sale. Then think about your own home and whether those items look very familiar. That may be enough motivation to start unloading some treasures. Then when you decide to move, it will be a much easier task.

CHAPTER 4

*Think you're ready to jump into
the real estate market?*

Buying or Selling?—"thinkidover"

July Fourth usually provides a glorious holiday weekend. Banks close, government offices close and title companies close too. Besides reminding me of how nice long weekends are, it reminds me how important it is to take some time for reflection. When buying a home, you have to be careful to factor in this important step: time to think things over.

My dad had a great saying. Summer was a time when he seemed to use this saying a lot, especially when we were anxiously asking about going somewhere like the beach or a trip to the amusement park or out to our cousins' farm. Kids are not known to be patient, particularly during summer vacations. I can see him calmly sitting in his kitchen chair at the table and saying, "Hmmmmm, that's an idea; I'll have to 'thinkidover.'" Just like that. I guess he slurred those words together because we probably made him say them frequently. In his favor, he did "thinkidover," and we have a ton of great family memories to show for it.

The spring of 2021 real estate market tipped to a sellers' market. Of course that meant that sellers were no longer waiting and waiting for offers and then relisting their homes just to accept mediocre prices. Buyers were alert and making offers on homes more quickly. And we frequently saw more than one offer on homes. But even when a real estate market is hopping, buyers and sellers still need to take a breath, follow a thorough process and be absolutely sure that they "thinkidover" before signing on the dotted line.

We don't have to think back too far, 2008, to remember painfully that many buyers were moving too quickly and not adequately thinking

Leland with his grandfather, Zaide Shulman, learning the art of 'Thinkidover." When he understood the game, we added a timer.

through their goals. Here are some helpful guidelines when buying a property, whether it is residential or commercial.

- Visit it once, visit it twice and visit one more time. First impressions are very important, but when going in a second time buyers **always** say, "I didn't notice that." On the first walk-through, buyers look at rooms and sizes and general condition. Some get off track, peering up at family pictures, trying to identify the owners and figure out if they know anyone there. Then as we get back on track, they may go outside and wander. A first visit is obviously important, but you probably won't notice the missing floor trim. Or you may not see the chipping paint behind the bathroom door. Most first-time visitors won't be looking under the carpeting to check for hardwood floors either.

I remember a client calling me one evening after looking at a condo. She was washing dishes in her own kitchen, thinking about the condo, when she realized there was no dishwasher in that home or even a place to put one. Neither of us had caught this obvious void on our first trip. You can always revisit a home quickly. One visit one day and one visit the next. You don't have to wait a week, especially in a bustling market. Just be sure to go back and see the property you are buying as many times as possible.

- Read the paperwork and understand it. Real estate transactions have voluminous documents to read. A buy-sell agreement is 10 pages long, and disclosures can run over 10 pages also. Then there are attachments and subdivision plats, inspections and appraisals and title reports. All the details are part of the whole transaction and cannot be hurried.

I had a less than flattering client say to me, "Well, this isn't rocket science. Anyone can do this work." While it is true that real estate is not quantum physics, I thought about this annoying comment some more. Recently I watched "Apollo 13," starring Tom Hanks. This spellbinding movie reminds us all, once again, that the devil is in the details. Missing one contact in an oxygen tank had the world holding its breath for the astronauts' safe return. Missing a line in the buy-sell paperwork or missing the understanding of a disclosure form could mean that you end up owning a property that doesn't have an adequate septic system or a property that has a history of mold. Or the rental you are buying has an ongoing lawsuit you are taking on. While a buyer may not equal an astronaut trying to come back to Earth, it might feel that way to you if you end up buying something you didn't bargain for. Read and understand *all* the paperwork. If there is anything you don't fully understand, ask your agent or attorney to explain it **before** you sign.

- Enjoy the process. Look up, look around and take stock of the entire situation. You should always step back and make sure you are headed in the right direction. It's important to trust your instincts as part of this process. It involves complicated decision-making, but it should be exciting and enjoyable too. Moving forward, for most people, can be nerve-racking. However, there should be elements of knowing that this is the direction where you wish to head. This is where a team process helps to remind you of your goal. In spite of paperwork and visits and tons of conversations, it is going to be a great move forward for the right reasons. Remember to enjoy it all along the way.

Buying a home is not something you want to do every few years. It should be an exciting part of your life, a time to venture into new territory whether you are in a new town or just a new environment in the same town. Wherever you may go, be sure that each step of the way you take the time (not too much but just enough) to "thinkidover."

Stay Focused—Don't Get Hung Up on Irrelevant Things

B uying a home at the right time is personal. A young couple may be choosing the first place they will share as a duo. A growing family may be moving into a bigger home to accommodate a newborn. And an aging couple may decide it is time to sell and find a less demanding house. People choose to sell their homes and buy others for various reasons that matter only to themselves. Then why do buyers ask why sellers are selling? Why do sellers need to know about the future occupants of their home? When it comes time to move, sellers and buyers must be coached that selling is strictly a business deal. Personalities and personal issues have ruined many real estate transactions that could have reached satisfying conclusions. Instead, the parties involved wasted time, money and stress thinking about irrelevant things out of their control. They learned the hard way not to mix business with nosiness. Sellers end up selling their homes for less, and buyers miss out on homes they really want.

The key to a real estate transaction is *focus*. Just as in sports, keep your eye on the ball and forget about the crowd cheering or booing. A motivated seller is a person who is ready to move on to another living arrangement. They need to know what their home will sell for in the current market and how long it may take. Some people are right on track. They paint, clean and pack up their home, staging it for a quick sale. Then the day comes when an offer to purchase arrives. There is rejoicing until they see the amount offered is way below the asking price. At this point, the sellers may get angry and take it personally. On several occasions, I have seen sellers Google buyers to learn more about them. They usually aren't speaking with the buyers at that point, so the mounting anger is inward and maybe toward their real estate agent. While reading this, it's easy to see the mistake. It doesn't really matter who the buyers are. There may not be a second chance to realize that it isn't about the people—it's a business deal. Keeping a level head can be tough.

Buyers and sellers get hung up on details that don't matter. They regard the transaction in terms of who is winning and who is losing. Many years ago, I worked with a woman I'll call Sarah. She owned a historic home that was beautifully restored. Sarah hadn't lived there for more than five years, but she took great pride in her home. When she decided to sell for personal reasons, Sarah wished for a new owner to preserve and enjoy the house as she did. After the home was listed, two buyers came forward to make offers, one substantially higher than the other. The lower offer was from a younger couple who expressed a desire to raise their family there and occupy it for the long term. The higher offer, more desirable both monetarily and in terms of an easy closing, came from a person she didn't know anything about. Sarah sold it to the younger couple because she felt she was helping them out. However, they quickly sold the home again for a tidy profit. It was obvious their story was disingenuous. I probably don't need to say more about this story. Sarah's comments are not fit for print.

Most of the time, when you are ready to sell a home, a property, a business—move forward. Don't get bogged down in trying to understand buyers. Selling a home is enough work. Don't worry about people you will probably never know or understand.

On a lighter note, after trying hard to get across the idea of keeping emotions at bay, sometimes interjecting personal issues can help. Once I was negotiating for a seller who sincerely wished to sell. And the buyers loved the home, but the purchase price could not be reached. Along with the stress of negotiations, the seller was concerned about his pet. He had a cat that took pride in mouse maintenance, and he was sure his cat wouldn't move easily. Finally, he said if the buyers would let the cat stay, he would agree to the deal. It was something that really mattered to him, that was personal and that made the final agreement happen. Sometimes it's the smaller issues that *can* make a difference. Leave that load of firewood; share expenses for cleaning up the yard, repairing the broken fence and scrubbing the house spick-and-span. Don't get petty. If you give a bit, the entire deal will go much smoother and you will be on your way.

Real estate deals move forward when you work on the key factors affecting the sale. Keep an eye on those important issues. Selling a home is a business deal that can help you achieve the next goals in your life. Don't try to interpret other people's motives. Give a little or a lot, if it makes you feel better. But don't get hung up on details that really don't matter.

Pitfalls of Buying and Selling—Be Cautious

I nevitably, if you become involved in real estate, you will hear a miserable story about something you hope never happens to you. By the time we get to this point in our lives, we often figure that we can recognize a situation that is too good to be true. And, of course, we know that if it seems to be too good to be true, there is probably a catch.

If you are buying, selling or helping someone in their real estate endeavors, you should know how to recognize the pitfalls of real estate transactions. If you start out with that attitude, the rest should go according to plan most of the time.

Here is one of my first encounters with an unpleasant real estate experience, which happened early in my marriage during a vacation:

My husband, Mark, and I were on a fun road trip during a two-week vacation from work. We hadn't been married long and were becoming used to each other's travel habits. We were visiting friends and also spending days exploring new places on our own. After a stay in San Francisco, it was time to start back to Missoula. Neither one of us had been to Lake Tahoe, so we stopped there for the night.

Upon checking into our room, we were offered a free dinner, money and an exciting ride to a new resort. It sounded like fun. Free food, money and new sights were enticing offers to a young couple with a small budget.

Well, it sounded great to me. Mark insisted that it was too good to be true, and we had a limited time to enjoy this town. I thought it might be an adventure to visit someplace we wouldn't ordinarily get to see. I guess we were both right in some ways.

We told our "tour guides" that we could not even consider buying anything at this new resort, and they insisted that it didn't matter. We boarded a bus (first mistake) and headed up a mountain. The bus either broke down or ran out of gas. I am still not sure. But we stayed on the side of this steep road for eternity until another bus came.

At this point, we were hungry, and when we finally arrived, we thought our tour guides would provide dinner to their guests. Instead, they showed us some luxurious homes that we couldn't even comprehend. They were expensive, and we couldn't even afford a house in Missoula. After what seemed like hours, a woman brought us into another room. She started interrogating us about our finances, our lifestyle and our habits. We looked at each other; we weren't sure how to respond.

I knew what Mark was thinking, and I just wanted to disappear. With a smile, I politely asked where dinner was or the bus to go down this imposing mountain. I only remember her long fingernails tapping on the table, perhaps in hopes that we were going to magically turn into another couple with money. I really don't know.

The rest is a blur except that when we finally returned to town, in the dark, Mark and I agreed that we had just observed another world that we did not want to re-enter.

That was a long time ago, and I believe many people have had the same experience we did. Why don't we learn from them and from each other? We really should.

Here are some pitfalls you can recognize, protect yourself from and prepare yourself for in case you find yourself in these situations.

If you are buying a home or assisting someone buying a home, here are some things to consider:

- Ask questions. You should become concerned if sellers are slow to respond, if they don't know obvious answers or if they are annoyed by your inquiries.

- Don't ignore your gut feelings. If something doesn't feel right about a property, you may be subconsciously observing an issue or problem that you can't put your finger on yet. Sometimes it just makes sense to walk away.

- Do not let your emotions get the best of you, and always remember that you will find what you are looking for eventually. I remember being told that I would never find all the things I was looking for in a home. I didn't believe those words and did find the best spot, and you will too.

If you are selling, here are some important things to ask buyers:

- Are they qualified to buy your home? Ask for verification before you go too far in the process of working with the buyers. If they act annoyed or confused, then slow down and don't move forward. If they want to lease or rent prior to purchase, ask the same questions. Verify that they have the funds to adequately assure you they will follow through on what they are telling you they will do.

- Do not let someone you haven't thoroughly identified into your home. You must know who they are so that you don't put yourself in a dangerous situation. Criminals and shysters will take advantage of your good nature and the fact that you want to sell. They know that kind, honest people don't feel comfortable calling someone a liar. I know this is blunt, but it can save you some serious problems.

When you are ready to sell, you can often easily overlook obvious or uneasy feelings. Don't do it. It never hurts to slow a process down, ask for assistance and verify facts. In the end, you may find that you are just being overly cautious, but it is better than not taking precautions.

I have observed sellers move out of their homes under quick and stressful conditions only to find out that the buyers couldn't do what they said they could. Like Mick Jagger and the Rolling Stones said, "Time is on my side, yes it is."

Whether you are buying or selling real estate or helping someone you know, step back and observe. Is this process going along the way it should? Are there signs that something isn't right, but you don't know exactly what? Then there probably is something else happening. Find out what it is before going any further.

Remember me, sitting on that bus on the side of the mountain in Lake Tahoe. It was a long way up and a long way down. I was hungry and tired at the end and didn't have much to show for the experience. Selling or buying real estate should not be this kind of adventure.

Hidden Costs When Buying or Selling—'Not the Rabbit Ears!'

A spring real estate season is undeniable.

Activity picks up. Sellers who debated whether to list their homes enter the market. Others make finishing touches and decide on a suitable time to list. Potential buyers start going to open houses, and serious ones make offers.

We could debate the reasons for this activity: Perhaps people are tired of waiting to buy or sell; perhaps we had more blue sky over winter; perhaps we can't imagine interest rates ever being lower or staying this low for so long; or perhaps it's an election year. Whatever the reason, buyers and sellers take action and make offers. This is what I want to talk about in today's column.

If you have decided to finally jump into the real estate market, either as a buyer or a seller, you will be involved in a negotiation at some time — sooner rather than later, I hope. This means you have either offered to purchase a property or have received an offer. How do you respond now? Let me share an experience I will never forget. I recount this story as it happened to my husband and me when we were in our 20s.

In 1979, Missoula was in a deep recession, along with most of the country. There was no work anywhere except in eastern Montana and North Dakota, where the oil boom was in full swing. Mark and I packed up some belongings, drove out east and were fortunate to find work quickly. I was hired on with an engineering firm, and Mark started working on an

'The rabbit ears' live in a prominent spot at our home. They remind us that the smallest of details can make a big difference.

oil rig. Things clicked along well, and we were able to move out of a tent camp to a mobile home duplex. That was deluxe.

On a day off work, we visited a secondhand store to purchase a few items for our home. When we walked into the shop, the owner was watching a TV show. Although we weren't big television watchers, we asked what it would cost to purchase the set. The amount was reasonable, so we offered to buy it. After we paid, Mark picked up the television, but the shop owner said to wait a moment. We had purchased the TV, but not the rabbit ears. Older TVs did not come with built-in antennas, essential for tuning in stations in 1979 North Dakota. Rabbit ears attached to the top of television sets had a base that looked like the top of a head with two adjustable antennas sticking out of it like alien's ears. By moving the two ears around, you could hopefully get a clear picture of your desired station. The store owner knew we could not use the television without the rabbit ears, so he requested another $4 in addition to the initially agreed upon $20 for the set. We paid the entire $24, and the TV worked fine during our stay in Williston.

The day came when we had saved enough money and were ready to return to Missoula. Since we didn't need to bring a TV all the way back home, Mark returned to the little secondhand shop. The owner was happy to buy back the TV, at a lower price than we had paid. We understood, as he had a business to run. Mark put the television on the counter and collected our money. Then Mark remembered. He started unscrewing the rabbit ears. The shop owner asked what he was doing. Mark said he had offered to buy back the television, but not the rabbit ears. There was no dispute. And to this day, we still have those rabbit ears. They remind us of our youth, and they remind us about our first negotiation lesson.

When a deal turns out to be different than we expected, around our house we often say, "Not the rabbit ears." Everyone knows what that means and now you do, too.

I hope you find yourself negotiating to buy or sell a property at some point. It is an important step in the process. While price is a key factor, there can be hidden costs that you want to discover before you complete negotiating. It will save you time, money and possible frustration. Too often, after a contract is in place and the parties are ready to conclude the transaction, small details become very important. I have heard of deals falling apart over seemingly insignificant things. (These stories are for another column.)

Buying or selling a property should be an enjoyable process, but for too many people, it can be unreasonably stressful. Spend the important time reviewing the details. And please, don't forget the rabbit ears.

CHAPTER 5

*If an egg and a half costs
a penny and a half, how much does
a dozen eggs cost?*

Gather a Team—Seek Professionals
Who Know Their Business

Spring brings out many kinds of buyers. Those contemplating buying in the future, those considering selling their home to purchase a new one, and people just having fun looking at houses while quietly considering a new home. I work with all types. Home shopping is overwhelming, time-consuming, and sometimes feels like there are just too many things to think about. If you don't whittle down your choices, you will never move forward, which is OK if you enjoy looking at homes. But if you truly need to make a move, you need a plan.

I know how it can feel when you are inundated with buying choices you haven't had to analyze in the past. One winter, our son Leland asked us if we wanted to meet him in Colombia. We said yes, with little hesitation. How often does your son offer up an adventure like that? The day before we were leaving, my friend Roger adamantly said that I had to buy emeralds, as they were prolific there. Buy emeralds? I think I have owned one in my lifetime, which is on my engagement ring. I love it, but I didn't really pick it out. Hunting one down would be fun, and I am always up for a challenge. Plus I knew Roger would inquire about my thorough search-and-find mission. Before we left, another friend, Michelle, asked me to pick one out for her too. It seemed like fun, something new that I didn't know much about.

Mark and I found the emerald district in Bogotá without too much trouble. Shop after shop, vendor after vendor waved us in their direction as we walked into the district. Most don't speak English, but they had calculators that showed Colombian pesos that are thousands to one of our dollars. My son Leland had primed me to learn my numbers, so I felt pretty good about that. After aimless strolling, it all blurred together. Occasionally, a gorgeous green glow would catch my eye, and I quickly learned that those were the ones that had far too many zeros after two or three numbers on the calculator. I didn't need my math skills for that. Mark was patient over the next few hours. But when I looked over at him, I saw that he knew before I did that we were never going to figure this out. I am not a gem buyer. I could sort through them vaguely, and I sure recognized the fabulous ones. But to make a smart purchase, I needed a mentor.

Over a lifetime of buying, I have tried to learn from the people who either work in a specific field or study it closely. When I buy produce, I ask Paul, who has been a produce manager for decades at a local store. When I buy mutual funds, I ask a trusted adviser who knows the market and my needs. But in Colombia, when I wanted to buy an emerald, I had no one to assist with understanding the local market. After a day of shopping, I concluded I wasn't going to discover a fabulous gem at a bargain-basement price. I didn't have the skills or knowledge.

JONAGOLD APPLES $1.99 LB

GALA APPLES $1.99 LB

GRANNY SMITH $1.99 LB

Which is the better deal? I need to ask Paul, my produce consultant.

Buying a home is a process that takes experience and skill, like buying quality emeralds. You should surround yourself with helpers, guides and professionals. And break the process into logical steps. The first step is to understand what you wish to accomplish. Be honest with yourself and whomever you may be purchasing the home with. Are you looking or are you buying? This simple question and frank answer will save lots of discussions.

Next, if you are buying, start narrowing down the field. Otherwise, it will look like that blur of green did to me. Don't miss out on something great by wasting time looking at homes that aren't remotely appropriate. First narrow your search to a realistic price range and location. Take the time to truly understand your finances and neighborhoods. Bring in trusted advisers to assist with your search. At the same time, run numbers showing true costs.

Soon, you will start seeing a pattern. Now compare what you want with what is available on the market. Discuss the options with your team. Ask your advisers to be direct and honest, to furnish tried-and-true data, and to be willing to work with you for the long haul. This will allow you to enjoy the process and make it less of a chore.

Most people buy only three to five homes in their lifetime, and five is a lot. Each one should have a great story that goes along with the purchase. The only way to accomplish this is to have the right attitude, and clear communication with your team and yourself. When the right choice arises, it should be apparent. It will fit your list of criteria, you will feel as if a light bulb popped on and you will be ready to move forward.

Once you find your top choice, there are steps you must follow before closing on the home. But this first process of seeking out your future home should be carefully planned and followed. If you start out with the right advisers and the right plan, you will reach your goal.

For some people, buying a home can be like a trip to a foreign country. There is a different language to negotiate with a litany of choices that may be new. On my recent trip, when I was overwhelmed by the green glow of emeralds, I had the option to walk away. I happily settled into a local café and enjoyed a snack of delectable green figs and wonderful Colombian coffee. You should be clear about your home-buying options. Missoula is also filled with great places to enjoy a delicious cup of locally roasted coffee while you plan your next move.

Hone Your Math Skills — Know Your Costs

Hone your math skills. I guarantee that some of the simplest exercises will save you time, money and, best of all, peace of mind. This is especially true in any aspect of real estate, whether it is buying, selling, remodeling, refinancing or paying taxes.

My husband and I grew up hundreds of miles apart, yet our grandfathers had the same lessons to teach us. They would gather the grandchildren and quiz us with riddles. Our family favorite is this one: If an egg and a half costs a penny and a half, how much does a dozen cost? Did you know this answer quickly? Do you know it yet? Not to leave out our grandmothers' wisdom, I remember watching them make treats and ask how many cups to a quart, if you only have a teacup to measure it with. There are so many riddles that not only teach us the value of a dollar but teach us how easily we can be tricked or fooled by confusing situations involving numbers.

Selling real estate is a complicated process. Some homeowners, when considering selling, start with what might be considered the basic numbers. They sometimes have a real estate specialist or appraiser calculate the approximate value of their home if it were to sell on the market within the next six months. They might even take the next step in considering the costs for preparing their home for sale. Those seem like simple calculations and evaluations. But are they really?

Let's review some possible costs that might not be readily apparent. Here is a simple example: Your home definitely needs new carpeting. Should you replace it to sell your home? You go to the store and find that carpet costs so much per square yard. Then you can have it installed by the full job or per hour. How much does it cost per square foot to install your carpet? That's a relatively easy task, but think of the time involved in pricing, getting quotes and then trying to evaluate the best value. We didn't even discuss the type of carpeting or quality of the installer.

After all that, some people might say it isn't worth changing the carpet and decide to let a buyer choose what carpet they prefer when they purchase it. That is a seemingly easy solution. That simple decision can cost extra money because the home might be on the market longer and expenses mount every month. An owner must understand all those expenses and figure out the true costs incurred each month a home doesn't sell.

Now, let's get a little more complicated. Some owners choose to sell their homes "For Sale by Owner." At first thought, the math seems simple. Full commissions don't have to be paid to real estate brokerages. These sellers sometimes offer commissions to real estate agents who bring buyers. On the surface, the homeowners feel like they are saving money. But how much does that egg and a half really cost? Adding up costs to selling a home involves much more than commissions and new carpeting. The home has to be prepared, buyers need to know the home is for sale, a sign must go up, advertisements must be placed and calls must be answered. That's the easy part. The tasks and time continue with showings, long conversations with prospective buyers and information sharing. There are actual costs and true expenses involved in every step of this process.

However, the hidden costs or savings can come next. In most home sales, negotiations ensue, then there are inspections and closing costs. Just as in carpeting and painting expenses, these can add up faster than anyone could imagine. Along the way, there are significant steps that, if not calculated properly, can feel like a rotten egg was hidden in the dozen. No one wants to even think about potential liabilities or lawsuits over mis-communications along the way.

Intertwined throughout all this information are invariably mathematical calculations. Which is a better deal in the following situation? In the first scenario, you are offered a large down payment as a deposit and then will collect rent until a buyer has completed the financing in three months. In a second scenario, you are offered a cash settlement but need to wait six months until the final sale. Now, add some other factors, such as this was your primary residence for three of the past six years and your spouse needs expensive medical care. The carpet example seems so darn simple when you add taxes, Medicare and moving to the mix.

Our grandparents had so much to teach us through all their experiences. They were immigrants, they were poor and they persevered. So what was one of the most powerful lessons they chose to teach us? What you hear and what you think you hear might not be the true cost to you. Listen, think and hone your basic math skills.

A Real Estate Quiz

Real estate is a topic everyone is interested in at one time or another. It makes for great discussion at dinner parties, chance meetings at supermarkets or around the water cooler at work.

Sometimes it seems like everyone wants to know if houses are selling or people are buying. Then the speculation begins about whether it's due to higher interest rates or a recent drop in gas prices or a tornado in one part of the country and a flood in another. Everyone has a thought or an opinion. I recall an economist once said that he wouldn't want to lose a hand because then he'd never be able to say: "on the other!"

To be ready for that next real estate conversation or if you will be entering the real estate market, I put together a quiz to hone your knowledge. Multiple choice seemed like more fun. Try to find the best answer or pick several if you think more than one applies, or answer "none of the above" if you don't like any of the choices. Then see what I say below.

---

1. What is a Realtor?

    A. A member of the NAR

    B. A member of the NRA

    C. A person licensed to sell real estate

2. What is a real estate broker?

A. A type of real estate license as defined by state codes

B. A licensed real estate agent with their own office

C. Someone who can supervise other real estate agents

3. Do all real estate brokers charge the same commission?

A. Yes, there is a scale to determine charges

B. No, it is up to individuals

C. Sometimes within and between offices

4. Will I save money if I sell my home myself?

A. Always, as there is no commission to pay

B. Sometimes, as you may still pay a commission

C. It depends on the circumstances

5. Is an appraisal required when selling a home?

A. It depends on the circumstances

B. Yes, it is always required

C. No, it is not required

6. Is there a better time during the year to sell a home than another?

A. Yes, always in the early spring

B. Yes, always in the late spring

C. No, not really

7. **If I have a home for sale at $300,000 and get an** offer **the first day at $290,000, should I take the offer right away or wait?**

    A. No, don't take it; it's only the first day and you could get more

    B. Maybe, as it depends on how you priced your home

    C. Yes, take the money and move on

8. **Should I replace the carpeting and paint my home prior to selling?**

    A. Always, as you will get the money back when you sell

    B. Sometimes

    C. Never, as people like to pick their own colors

Answers

1. *A and C* are both required. A Realtor is a trademark name that applies to members of the National Association of Realtors. Members must meet all requirements required by the state to become a licensed real estate agent. However, real estate agents can practice without belonging to the National Association of Realtors, but they cannot call themselves Realtors. The NAR requires members to adhere to specific standards, including codes of ethics. Membership also provides benefits.

2. *A.* A real estate broker in the state of Montana must first become a licensed real estate agent. Then, after a specific number of years of practice, engaging in a specific number of transactions, taking additional training and passing an exam, an agent may obtain a broker's license. This does not mean they have their own office. In order to supervise other agents, a broker must also obtain a supervisory endorsement requiring additional training and continuing education. Brokers must sign all listing and real estate contracts. Real estate agents must work under supervisory brokers at all times.

3. *B.* Brokers engage in listing contracts with their clients. Commissions are based on what is agreed upon in their contract. Typically, listing brokers will share this commission with other brokers who are representing buyers. Brokers and offices are not permitted to set specific commission rates together as that would be price-fixing.

4. *C.* It is always advisable to compile a "net sheet" with your costs on selling your home. Very often, when people choose to sell homes by themselves, hoping to save money, they are surprised at the costs in the end. Some of these include marketing and advertising, signage, commissions to buyer's agents, charges to place ads online and on real estate signs, losses in negotiations, contract information they are not trained for and other unknown fees. The big cost can be potential lawsuits, as in latent material facts about the home. Homeowner's insurance may not cover lawsuits that arise from a sale. Carefully calculate the costs with someone who knows them and then decide. Simply pricing your home wrong in the first place can lose more money in the end than you realize.

5. *A.* Lenders require appraisals to assure that their loan is backed by a property worth its value. Real estate buyers not obtaining a loan don't usually need an appraisal, but it's not a bad idea as it is informative and useful for tax purposes.

6. *C.* Trying to time the market in real estate is like timing the stock market. If you are off by even a day, you may lose a great buyer. And you only need one good buyer. So the key is to prepare your home for sale and put it on the market when you are ready. There are peaks and troughs all year long and some surprises for even the analysts. You are not a speculator. You are in this for your life choices. Make the decisions for your personal reasons, and it will be the right decision.

7. *B and C.* An offer depends on more than the monetary amount. You will want to make sure the buyer can perform, which takes some analysis. We learn in real estate that often (not always) the first offer will be the best. Or at least the first buyer will be the one who is the most motivated, so the first offer is a good place to start negotiations. Don't be too quick to say you don't really need to sell that fast. It may be a long wait for the next offer, and it may not be nearly as good.

8. *B.* You can never be guaranteed that you will get your investments back when you carpet or paint or do repairs prior to selling. But first impressions are everything. So if there are serious odors or very particular colors (your daughter's pink bedroom she insisted on when she was eight), it may be a good idea to remedy those. Get some honest opinions. You should consider minor repairs. Leaky faucets and dried up yards don't give the right message to potential buyers.

How did you do? There are so many questions about real estate. If you are going to dive into the market it is important to know some of the basics.

First-Time Buyers—Put a Process in Place

Personal handwritten mail has become more of a rarity, so recently when I opened my mailbox, I instantly recognized a letter that was meant just for me. This wedding announcement brought memories, smiles, excitement and heartfelt happiness. I opened it while walking down my driveway and stopped as I read that the reception was to be at the couple's home in Missoula. I could picture the beautiful yard and guests enjoying a treat under the shade of their maple tree. I have known Conor, the groom, since he was born. I met his fiancé, Rose, as we searched for homes and shared Thanksgiving time together. They are both hometown Missoulians, born and raised here. It was a treat and honor to be involved in this part of their lives. This is how our adventure worked and almost didn't happen.

First, I suppose, many people wouldn't consider a home search as an adventure. But they should. After all, just as it was with Conor and Rose, looking for a place where you will enjoy your life, family and future is exciting in that respect alone. It takes work and perseverance. That is what I enjoyed so much with this young couple. They were ready to roll up their sleeves, learn the process and make house-hunting goals. Conor has always been very conscientious, so I wasn't surprised that he had saved money for a good down payment. He met with several lenders and was ready to go, all preapproved. So many new house hunters make the mistake of looking at homes before they know how much of a home they can buy or if they are even eligible to purchase. Starting out that way is frustrating and a waste of time for everyone involved. I have seen homes under contract where the deals fall apart after the buyer finds out he is not even qualified. The sellers are not only upset but have potentially missed out on buyers who could have moved ahead and bought their home. It is an upsetting, huge disappointment that is completely avoidable. When Conor and Rose found the right home, I knew they would be ready to make an offer.

We narrowed down our search online and set up a system to look at listings together that way. Then during their lunch breaks from work and in the evenings, we hit the ground running. Each day we all looked at homes that were newly posted on the market. We knew that as first-time home buyers, their competition could be fierce when an affordable home came on the market. We looked at tiny homes on busy streets. Then we looked at big rambling old homes. We looked at refurbished homes and those that were in foreclosure. Finally, we found one not far from Rose's parents' home that looked nice. We discussed and debated, but the price seemed a bit high, and it was an older home that we thought might be cold in the winter. As we were talking about all those details, the home went under contract. That was a good experience as Conor and Rose learned about how real estate markets really work.

At the time the press was saying it was a buyers' market, meaning that home sales were slow and buyers could probably take their time when making an offer on a home they wanted to buy. A buyers' market implies that prices are low or that offers can be made substantially lower than the asking price. This type of thinking can be a mistake and can confuse buyers. They may drag their feet and miss an ideal home. While it is OK to read generic articles about the real estate market, if you are truly ready to purchase a home, you need to educate yourself about the particular type of house desired in a specific location. You also need to methodically move forward and not try to play the market.

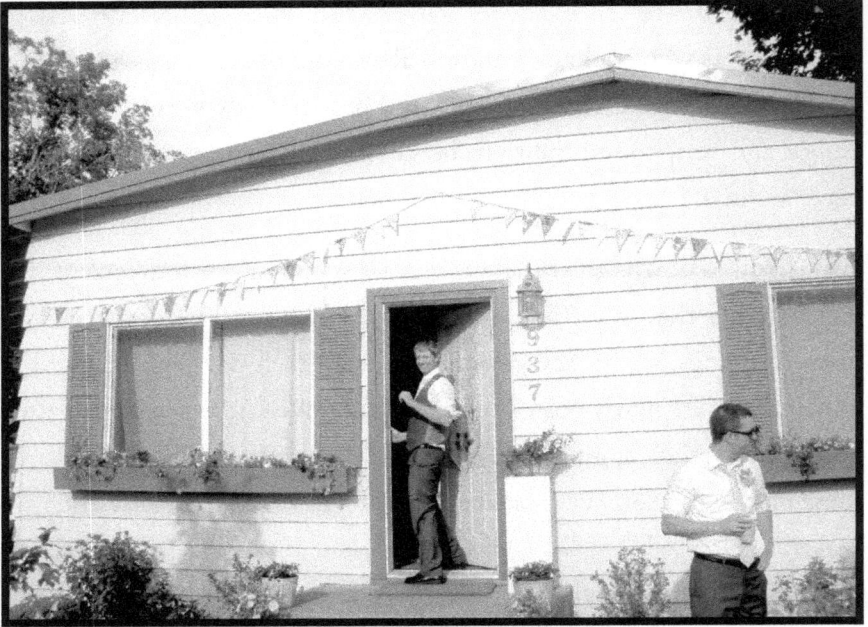

Conor on his wedding day. After they said their vows,
they hosted a reception at their new home.

For Conor and Rose, buying a home was a long-term commitment, as it should be. Their home will gain equity over the years, probably more than they imagine now. Just like many Missoula couples I know who have lived in their homes for many years, their home is now their biggest asset. And it certainly wasn't what was in their minds years ago when they signed up for their 30-year mortgage.

Back to their story. As you can guess, one morning, a great home popped up on our computers. I immediately texted Conor, as he was at work. He waited until his break (just in case his boss is reading this). We met at noon at the home, and then Rose came at 5:30, after her classes at the university. The decision was made to write the offer. Negotiations ensued, as did other buyers' offers, even in this buyers' market that the press kept talking about. Conor and Rose's offer was the one accepted. We celebrated! There were inspections, appraisals and final lender's underwriting.

As time went by, the seller began having second thoughts. After all, she had bought this home before she was married, later wed and had a beautiful daughter, whom we met on one visit to her home. This little girl proudly showed us her big tree in the yard and pointed at her friend's home across the street. Moving was going to be hard for them emotionally, and this seller almost backed out. But in the end, we continued to move forward with the purchase and did not make anything difficult for this seller. Conor and Rose closed on their home on schedule. And I have a great picture of them in front of their new home to show it!

Now this is the part of the story that Conor and Rose don't know. Mark and I still love to drive around Missoula looking at what is going on in different neighborhoods. One evening, after walking the dog through Caras Park downtown, I suggested we detour on our way home. Part of our circuit was past Conor and Rose's home. I spotted them sitting at their picnic table under the big shady maple tree. They seemed to be talking and writing, so we didn't want to disturb their quiet evening. Now, reading their wedding invitation as I walk from my mailbox, I think I know what they were doing.

CHAPTER 6

'Where did those purple
petunias on the deck go?
Wasn't that part of the deal?'

Getting Your Home Ready for
Sale—Staging and Photos

The internet is a critical tool to employ when marketing your home. However, remember that technology can be a huge asset if used properly but an enormous deterrent if you aren't mindful or skilled.

If you are gearing up to sell, pictures are a must for showcasing your home so that a buyer will want to make an offer immediately upon viewing. Remind yourself that these pictures feature your home for sale, not your life's accumulation of stuff.

I learned a lot about photographing homes after meeting Marilyn. She forever altered the way I look at homes when I first visit.

Marilyn has a business helping people to aggressively declutter their homes, which is how I first met her. To understand her skills, you have to meet Marilyn. She has been known to dress as a pink fairy and fly through houses with her magic wand, skillfully disappearing unsightly items. I don't know exactly how she does it.

The highlight of my day is when I see an email from her because I know she is sending me pictures she saw on the internet of an unpolished house that has just come on the market. Her insights and pointers are invaluable to me while I familiarize myself with a new listing. Her talents emerge and continue to grow as she surfs the internet and looks at photos of homes. I get the benefit of her knowledge and insight, and sometimes some good chuckles for the day.

A year or two ago, she sent me a link to a listing. Right there in the bathroom, the owner had her wash strewn about. This was more information than we wanted to know about this seller. I won't get into details about size and shape. (Did I mention zebra print?) Thankfully, these were clean clothes, not dirty ones on the bedroom floor.

Another homeowner prominently featured their cat strutting on the kitchen counter. Does he come with this house at no extra cost? We've had fun conversations about the people in the pictures, too. Did this woman in the picture realize she was a featured asset in this home? Is the cute guy in the yard included?

When you decide to sell your home, you want buyers to concentrate on the fabulous features you are selling, not your stuff. Take pictures of the home before you list your house for sale. Then look at them closely and critically. Here are some tips to keep in mind that Marilyn taught me:

- **For the kitchen:** Get rid of decorative items above and around cabinets, so you feature the cabinets, not the stuff. Clear off countertops. Pack stuff inside cupboards so you can remove your appliances from the counters. Take the tablecloth off the table.

- **For the bedroom:** Make the bed nicely with new linens and bedspreads. Clean off nightstands. Raise the curtains.

- **Some general tips:** No garbage in sight, ever. No animals in sight, ever. (That includes animal mounts, too.) No people or shadows in sight, ever. No decorations smaller than a football in sight, ever, as they look like clutter in photos.

I could list more, but the theme is clear. Keep it uncluttered and impersonal. Keep the focus on the house and its features.

Move managers like Marilyn get the tough
jobs done well while making it fun!

When a person first thinks about selling their home, they know they must clean and get it ready for pictures and showings to prospective buyers. But cleaning is not the same as decluttering. Photographing a home is an important element when marketing. Buyers need to focus on the architectural features of a home and not get sidetracked by looking at people, animals and some stranger's dirty dishes.

Be Cautious When Showing Your Home— Don't Get Sidetracked by a Thief

When someone begins the process of selling their home, they usually focus on trying to understand how to get it ready to show, how to figure out the price and, most important, how to get people in to see their home.

Sellers need to be cautious when showing their home to prospective buyers. Most people wouldn't think of inviting guests, or even friends, to view their closets, bedrooms or bathrooms. That would be extremely uncomfortable or embarrassing. So why do sentiments change when opening up a home to complete strangers who say they want to buy a home? Do they really want to buy a home, or are they just snooping around or even worse? This isn't meant to scare people, just to recognize potential problems before they arise. This occurred to me when I was thinking of an interaction I had this past year.

I received a call from another real estate broker working with an out-of-state client. The conversation was fairly rushed as she was obviously busy when she asked for my assistance. I agreed to work with her client, a buyer she didn't know very well. I called the woman right away. That conversation was also hurried, but she insisted she was serious, for her home in another state had just sold. She needed to buy a home quickly. She was in town and wanted to buy something right away in a very remote area. I gave her my office address, and we set a time to meet the next day. I immediately went to work, arranging properties to see and doing research. I was getting excited as I truly enjoy the challenge of helping someone find a great property. And she seemed appreciative. When I asked for her email, she said the other broker had it with her information. I wasn't sure why she didn't just give it to me, but I contacted the other broker and she sent me everything. My first red flag was the email address. It didn't look like one I had ever seen before, so I put that in the back of my mind.

The next morning, a Saturday, the buyer called and said she couldn't find my office. I asked her to stay where she was, and I met her in the parking lot of a fast-food restaurant. She had two dogs and her teenage daughter in the car. She was standing outside her van with the door open, sipping coffee out of a ceramic mug. I wasn't being nosy, but I couldn't help but notice big piles of stuff inside the van covering the dashboard and windshield. That was red flag number two. They looked like they had been living in this van for a period of time. Her license plates didn't match the state she said she was from or where she had just sold her property. I started a polite, chatty conversation to get to know her better and, frankly, to continue assessing this situation before we headed into the hills. I asked her where she had stayed the previous night, and she seemed forgetful until her daughter gave me the name of a hotel. I knew the hotel but asked them where it was, and they seemed confused. Again, in the back of my mind, I was going to check with the hotel when I got the chance.

My mind was racing, as I had already spent hours setting up showings and talking to agents and prospective sellers. But ignoring red flags, besides being a huge waste of time, can allow a bad situation to get even worse. I told her that I was not prepared to take two people and two dogs in my car all over Montana. That's what I said, but I was thinking that it wasn't a good idea for other reasons. What she said and what this looked like were not the same story. I politely reiterated that we weren't prepared for the day and would have to reschedule. She was agitated and not understanding at all. She asked me to send her all the property information or give her my files before I left. I haven't done either.

I immediately called the sellers of the homes we were going to visit. One home was being sold by the sellers personally. I cautioned them but also told them I did not give out their address or information. They said they hadn't even thought about the possible dangers of selling on their own without a professional representative. When I called the brokers and real estate agents for the other homes, they all thanked me. It is always better to cancel a showing if there are reasons to doubt the authenticity of a buyer. One agent told me her client was quite elderly and this would have upset her or could have caused untold problems.

When I reflect on this incident and other interactions I have had over the years, I can summarize some red flags to be aware of before letting people enter your home:

- Think about how you came to know these people — from the internet or from a closer source? Get their contact information, including home address, email and phone number, and verify them somehow. If they get upset, they are not worth working with.

- Get their lender information and contact them. If they say they are paying cash, get their banker's information. If it is the weekend, wait until Monday. If they get upset, they are not worth working with.

- Meet them in person in a public place, spend time there with them and observe body language. If they are uncomfortable, they are not worth working with.

- Make one or two phone calls, in front of the buyers, to people who will know where you are, and again watch the buyer's body language. If they are uncomfortable, they are not worth working with.

- Finally, try hard to forget that you really want to sell your home. Ask yourself if these people seem to be who they tell you they are. Are their words matching their actions? If you are uncomfortable, they are not worth working with.

Nice people — I am assuming that is you — don't want to hurt people's feelings, so you may be uncomfortable saying you won't let them in your home. People with ulterior motives will take advantage of that behavior. If this seems like overkill, I seriously advise that you use a professional to assist you in understanding a true buyer versus someone with other motives. After years of experience working with people in this manner, it becomes obvious most of the time.

Most people don't sell homes very often in their lives. They assume that callers are buyers seriously looking for new homes. Most of the time, this is true. However, sellers can get so excited that they overlook obvious signs of problems or something more serious.

This is exactly when danger can strike. Be sure to preapprove buyers before they come into your home. I remember that morning with this buyer, her daughter, two dogs and who knows what else in their van. It was a Saturday morning, and I still had time to enjoy a stroll at the farmer's market. I was enjoying my coffee when I bumped into a friend I had met years ago as a home buyer. We chatted and swapped stories. I was instantly reminded of what a true buyer sounds and looks like. It turned into a perfect morning and a perfect reminder to trust my instincts and spend more time enjoying Missoula.

The 'Earls' sign was on the home of Mark's youngest brother, Matt, and was gifted to us when he passed away.

Personal Property vs. Real Property—What Are You Selling?

A small package was crammed into our mailbox with the regular assortment of bills and flyers a few weeks ago. As soon as I got into the house, I threw it all on the counter and went immediately for the plump package with a return address from Illinois. Inside was a metal sign that said EARLS. There was even a small packet enclosed with little matching screws to hang it with. The note inside made me sit down. It was from Chris, my brother-in-law Matt's partner. Matt — Mark's youngest brother had passed away years before. Chris wanted us to put this sign on our home, as it had been on theirs for many years. Then he hoped we would someday pass it on to our boys for their home. Personal property is what makes a house a home. When you are selling your home, understand the differences between personal property and real property.

Most things screwed into a house are considered fixtures and part of the home being sold, real property. Personal property is things like your curtains and blinds. If you choose to keep fixtures, you must be very specific and let the new buyers know, in writing, what you are taking with you when you sell. Sometimes it's hard to discern what is a fixture and what is personal property. In those cases, I suggest sellers remove fixtures prior to showing their home for sale.

One time, I was representing a buyer on a large home with big decks wrapping around the house. Each time we visited the home, we walked out onto the deck, enjoying the views and the gorgeous flowers growing in the planters built along the railing. On the day of closing, the buyers and I went to the home for a last walk-through to make sure everything looked good. The deck looked unusually bare, and it didn't take us long to realize that the flower boxes were gone. Planters that we had thought were part of the bargain apparently were not, according to the sellers. My buyers were unhappy but easygoing about it. The house was lovely, and they would redecorate the deck. Now when I see planters, I look to see if they are physically screwed and attached to the home. Even if they are attached, I still include them as part of the sale, if the buyers expect them to stay. Be specific, even if something seems quite obvious.

Another time, during the purchase of a large commercial building, there was an electric fireplace against the wall in a waiting area. It had nice woodwork and was a warm and welcoming part of the property. Again, at the final walk-through prior to closing, the area looked bare and cold. The soothing, inviting fireplace was gone and the wall barren. In this case, it had never been discussed and was not part of the contract. It looked built into the entryway but was not. The nonprofit agency purchasing the property didn't argue, as the building was the most important factor. But I still think about that "cozy fireplace" when I walk into the building, as I frequently do. It should have been discussed. And I still think the fireplace should have been included.

Refrigerators, microwaves and stoves can all be moved out and are considered personal property. But what about the heater in the garage that can be unplugged and moved? What about the solar lights greeting guests in the dark? What about the sheds? What about the garden fences and hose holders? Or the sign heading into the shop specifying "man cave, enter at your own risk." What's included and what's going?

Sometimes you may want sellers to take something that they purposely leave. That could include woodpiles and debris around the home. It could mean the huge freezer from 1940 that doesn't look like it will fit through the door. You won't want to deal with it when you move in. Have the sellers take it when they go.

When you decide you are going to make an offer on a home, carefully walk through inside and out. Make note of what is part of the house, what is attached and what is not. Then be specific with the sellers. In your contract, write what is included in the sale and what must go. This is the time to negotiate with the sellers so you are all clear on what you are buying. When the sellers are moving, they won't have questions about what needs to be cleared out. And when you do your walk-through, you won't be upset about something missing. If there is personal property included in the sale and you are getting a loan, you will need a separate bill of sale to purchase the items. Lenders only intend to let you borrow money for the real estate and home, not to buy a lawn mower or the kid's swing set in the yard. It makes sense and is easy to write up the transaction if you plan it ahead of time.

The other day I was driving up to my home and saw the sign we had bought online years ago with the address of our house. It is parked amid an assortment of flowers that friends have shared with us from their yards over the years. I enjoy it when I pull in and just noticed that it perfectly matches the EARLS sign that Mark attached to the front porch by the door welcoming guests. I don't plan to sell our home anytime soon, but I know what's coming with us wherever we are headed.

Inspections—Important for Both Buyers and Sellers

I enjoy a bargain. Who doesn't? There is an exhilarating feeling when you are the one to unearth the best deal. However, there are times when it is not prudent to shave your dollars.

Instead, spending your money wisely can be an investment for the future. This is especially true in real estate purchases and the process you use when deciding to buy a particular home. Hiring a qualified home inspector is an insurance policy that will be money well spent.

Most people carry homeowner's insurance, and they sleep at night knowing if a disaster hits, they should be covered. But before you buy a home, it is even more important to know if there is a disaster hidden or waiting to happen. You may save yourself huge expenses if you don't buy a particular home because of something uncovered during an inspection. Remember, you can always walk away.

Deliberately moving forward step by step is critical to success. Once you find a home that fits your needs, you will want to be assured that there are no latent defects. A home inspector or person well versed in home construction can be your guard against long-term liabilities. Such people are also wonderful educators and can teach you how a home functions. The cost is minimal for the information gained. Don't skimp on this part of the home purchase. If you are considering saving a few dollars and not hiring an inspector, let me share a few stories first, then decide.

Do you need a home inspection? Why are you even wondering? Always hire a licensed inspector and ask them to give you a tour of the property and a summary when they're done.

I was working with a graduate student moving to Missoula to attend the university. He had saved his funds and was able to purchase a home he could share with roommates. He, his parents (as support) and I started the search. We found the perfect home, close to the university, with room for his needs and with an extensive remodel already completed.

I explained to him that the seller had completed an Owner's Disclosure Form to cover facts about the home. It is a form about four pages long that is typically completed by a homeowner, covering everything from the furnace to the roof. Many times an owner honestly may not be aware of an ongoing problem, and it won't be addressed on the form. Sometimes the owner may know of a past problem but omit it from the form for some reason.

In this case, the buyer reviewed each page and felt comfortable about his prospective new home. Next, he hired a home inspector and spent four hours looking over the home with the professional. Missoula is fortunate to have knowledgeable people to work with and the time was educational, informative and even fun until they looked into the attic. When they popped their heads into the space, it was evident that there was a black substance all over the boards. Upon the inspector's advice, we called a mitigation company, which confirmed our suspicions. There was mold in the attic. The problem was handled, and the house soon became this student's new home.

If he had tried to save some time or money along the way, he might be living in a home with problems. Then, at some time, when he decided to sell the home, he would have to work with a possibly more severe issue.

Many home inspectors are American Society of Home Inspectors-certified. They must meet certain qualifications and yearly training requirements, which keeps them current on issues like mold. Many of them can test for radon gas in a home and educate a prospective owner on acceptable levels. The inspectors whom I have come to know often have in-depth experience in the construction industry.

Many of my clients use their inspectors as great resources for information, from different roofing materials to roof trusses to foundation repair. Inspectors' purposes are not, in my mind, to point out obvious wear and tear on a home to try to get a seller to lower their asking price. Inspections should not be used as negotiation tools. Used in the proper manner, they are invaluable, even for the seller, in the long run. If you still aren't convinced of their value, here is another true story.

I had visited a home many times with a prospective buyer. She loved the home and was ready to move in right away. Of course, we slowed down and arranged for an inspection.

We originally visited the home during the winter. We had spent hours walking through and around this lovely brick home. It was vacant, so there was no furniture to obstruct views, and we really felt we knew this property. When I arrived on inspection day, the inspector had a very concerned look on his face. He walked us to an outside corner of the home, previously obscured by snow and ice. There was a crack that ran along the bricks and through the foundation. Something was happening to this portion of the home. A novice might not have seen this crack, but a trained eye, following professional inspection guidelines, wouldn't miss such a fracture.

What a value the price of that inspection seemed at that moment. Here was an insurance policy that paid off immediately. Although, in this case, my client didn't buy the home, it was still money well spent. And this buyer received a valuable education along the way.

After purchasing a home, you wouldn't forget to buy a homeowner's policy. However, the first "policy" that you might wish to buy is a thorough home inspection. You will have an informative report on your new home or perhaps know that it's time to keep looking for a different one.

CHAPTER 7

*Everyone needs a change at some
point—even Mom, Dad, and you.
Are there ideas out there that are worth
considering, but you haven't come
across them yet?*

The Perfect Mother's Day Gifts

The perfect Mother's Day gift, a house! A new house may seem like a ridiculous suggestion at first, but let's play around with that thought.

First I am going to offer some other ideas just in case you or someone you know, perhaps a son, needs some help making Mom smile on her special day. Mom might be your wife, your mother, grandmother or possibly your daughter. Whoever deserves a nice gesture, make it a great day for them.

A homemade card wins every time over a prewritten thought grabbed from the corner store. I have a hidden stack of handwritten notes I have collected over the years that I peek at when I need a little smile. My favorites are the colored pictures with our home featured somewhere, often with a dog or chicken or fish.

Our son Carter started a tradition of making cards, including his own coupons. I definitely cashed in on the ones offering help with cleaning. My favorites are "accompanying me to the store" and "getting hugs whenever I ask." I love how he sometimes signed them "Carter Earls," just in case I might confuse him with another Carter. This year, he will be home from college just in time for me to stock up on some of his coupons.

Conjuring up gifts you know Mom will appreciate during the year, when it isn't her special day, may be the best present of all. And anything related to home will be hard to beat, even if a completely new home isn't in the picture yet.

"A man's home is his castle." That's a phrase I know instinctively. Is there a women's counterpart? Probably, but I can't recite it off the top of my head. Mom's home may not be that idyllic right now. Think about it. There's always a list of chores to do. Whether it's vacuuming or dishes or spring cleaning, the castle may sometimes seem like it has too many chamber pots. Of course, husbands are there slugging away alongside wives. Still, the needs, responsibilities or wishes can often be different for each person. Certainly, kids can be oblivious to any of Mom's longings without a little prodding from Dad.

Here are some considerations, ideas and hints on what the mom in your life might enjoy on her special Sunday or any day.

My suggestion may seem like a riddle. What would the mom in your life wish for each day but never see with their eyes, only with their ears? The answer is not an answer but a question. Pose a question to the mom in your life. Make it formal by writing it in a card, but genuinely ask her what she wants, and it wouldn't hurt to present it over homemade pancakes and fresh-picked flowers. A family project will blast it out of the ballpark. I promise. Ask Mom what change she would like to see in the house. Be prepared, as this is supposed to be caring and from the heart. Let her dream a little or a lot. Even if you know that some of it won't happen this year or even next. She will love you for asking and listening and paying attention. To help you out, here are some things you might hear and what you may be able to do.

"I can't look at that kitchen floor anymore. It is dinged up and hard to clean." You can offer to hire a cleaner for the next few months and by Mother's Day next year, you will look into getting a new one.

"There's never an end to the piles of laundry." Offer to reorganize the laundry room with shelving and bins and a chalkboard that says whose turn it is to do the clothes for the week.

"I wish I had fresh veggies handy so we could eat healthier." Go outside with the kids and find a small spot or even a bucket. It really doesn't have to be a big project to show you care. Throw around some seeds and water them. It is pretty darn easy to grow lettuce. If you can't find the seeds, drive to a local farm and buy the plant. It doesn't get easier than that. Even if the project is a flop, she will enjoy the quiet in the house while you are all outside working on something just for her.

"I need some time, on a regular basis, for myself." Again, gather the troops and carve out a spot for Mom in the house. Make signs that say "Do not disturb" and write pledges to not bother her during certain hours or times of the week.

As I said earlier, prepare yourself for anything. There may be a larger and more looming question that you won't be able to answer as easily.

Mom might be thinking that her home just doesn't meet her needs anymore. It could be too large, too small, too many steps or in a different place than she wants to live now. Start the conversation with her. Put together a plan, even if it is very long range, but stick with it. You can set out a five-year plan to find and move to a home that better suits both your needs. Or plan to renovate your current home so that it will work for all of you.

Just one more piece of advice: Don't call your favorite Realtor to look at houses on Mother's Day, please. Leave that for Monday. (I have to put in a personal note for myself once in a while because this has happened more than once.) If Mom wants, you can go to open houses or surf the internet and start the house-hunting conversation that way.

Make Mother's Day a time to validate what Mom is genuinely thinking and where she wishes to be next year or the one after. One of the best gifts for Mother's Day is to ask the mother in your life what she really wants. I guarantee she will have some answers for you. The first time you try this, as Carter did for me, you may want to use your full first and last name. She will love you for asking and want to be sure she heard it right. That is the first step. She may then ask for a little time to reflect. In other words, step back and give the mom in your life some space to appreciate her caring clan.

A True Story About a Mom and Her Family—Think About the Reality

What is the best part about being a boomer? For me, it is going through life's challenges and changes, knowing so many other people are doing the same. Everywhere you look, boomers are changing the way we do things. Our generation has names for food, names for communicating, names for recreating and names for each other that are unique.

Real estate needs and changes are a central theme for us. I rarely meet a boomer who doesn't have a real estate story. We look around at our current homes and are becoming tired of the maintenance, work and upkeep on a property that is hard to part with for different reasons. Some of us want to keep our houses for children and their growing families. There is a sentimental attachment and the realization that, once we part with it, we are also saying goodbye to a full phase of our lives.

These thoughts are often whirling through our minds. But then we get a call or make a visit that stops us in our tracks and changes everything. A parent suddenly takes a turn for the worse and needs some help. Our thoughts about our own needs become diverted, with the present challenge of helping our parents.

I recently heard a story about a daughter who lived in Missoula, where she grew up and where her mother still lived. Her siblings lived out of state. As her mom needed more help to stay at home and maintain her independence, the assumption was that the daughter in town, Shirley, would bear the brunt of the work. Mom wanted to stay in her own home, and the siblings felt this should be possible, with help. Not only did Shirley all of a sudden have the responsibility of caring for Mom, but Mom's older home needed a lot of care as well. It didn't take long before Shirley was calling her brother and sister more often, describing how their mom was becoming frustrated. She was unhappy about her circumstances and losing independence each day. These siblings weren't prepared for this eventful day.

As boomers are living longer, so are our parents. Siblings, often living in different places, are faced with how to help our aging parents with mounting health and home issues. It may start with raking the leaves and cleaning out the gutters. But assisting our parents soon morphs into more and more tasks. Shirley's case is common, where the closest sibling is given this daunting task. But just living nearby does not mean that they have the skills to manage Mom or Dad's lives as well as their own. Even if they actually have that capacity, is it fair for brothers and sisters to expect the nearby sibling to take on those demands?

For Shirley and her family, the pressure became so intense that Shirley moved away, which wasn't an easy decision. After seeking the help of a counselor she realized that by neglecting her own needs she had become increasingly ill. The counselor advised her to say no to her mother and family. This major choice, a difficult decision, helped save her marriage and her life. Many people reading this might say that they would never do that. They couldn't move from their parents in a time of need even if it compromised their health and lives.

Her mom sold her home and moved into a new one, where she had an assisted living arrangement. This would never have happened if Shirley hadn't been assertive with her siblings and made a positive step for her own future.

This is a tough story to hear. We all like to think that we are more pro-active than Shirley's family. And we like to think that we are empathetic with our siblings. But a house is a large investment, and it is a big decision to sell a home that someone has lived in for many years. Boomers are faced with considering not only their own homes and needs, but often more immediately, their parents' homes.

A parent's home, the family home, is often the key to your parent's future. The equity they have built up over the years can finance their future needs, which can help provide for them comfortably as their needs increase. This can be accomplished in many ways, depending on the unique circumstances, including selling the home outright, obtaining a reverse mortgage, setting up a home equity line of credit, placing the home in a trust and more. Home equity can not only provide for your parents' future comforts but assist in upgrading and/or maintaining the home so that it will retain value when it finally comes time to sell.

This discussion should be at the top of the list when families get together. So plan this now for a reunion, Thanksgiving or any time your family has plans to meet. Sit down together and agree that if one sibling is in the same town, there will be no assumptions about who will carry all the mounting workload. These tough discussions should include the home and property, money issues, the car, the will and anything else Mom or Dad wants to talk about.

It might be worth hiring a facilitator, nurse case manager or social worker for a couple of hours. That way you will have a predetermined time to meet and discuss these important issues. You will also have an objective person, outside the family, to help you through some tough conversations and decisions. Then afterward, you can all go back to watching a good game on TV, sharing a favorite family treat and blissfully ignoring the changes that are looming.

When everyone goes back to their lives, you can have some assurance that at least you took the first step. It is hard enough to decide on changes for yourself. Finally, if you reach the point where you may be ready to make a move, your parent(s) might also need you. Talk with your siblings and parents. You can at least start a plan by opening the conversation. This will place you all in a better position to deal with your own lives and help one another at the same time.

Boomers have created some great resources related to this topic. Some of the material in this article was from *Home Instead* at www.homeinstead.com

Live With a Support System in Place—Independently at Home

When we think of Dad and our homes, many stereotypes come to mind. Dad's the one mowing the lawn until one of the children is old enough to want to do it and young enough not to protest too much. Dad's the one off in the shop, basement or garage tinkering with something, probably just finding his quiet place. Dad's the one with his head under the sink fixing an annoying drip. Dad is the one stretched out in the den or living room yelling at the screen with his favorite team playing. We know where to find Dad in our home, and it's where we expect him to be.

Time has a way of slipping by, and there may be subtle changes at first, then more obvious. Dad may need to take a break before finishing the lawn care, or he may still tinker in the garage but the projects take a little longer; the drip might be dripping for a while, and the time stretched out in the den may seem more frequent. That's certainly not a problem or cause for concern, but a hint to start thinking about long-term planning. Moving is not the only answer to dealing with necessary house maintenance. There are many choices today, but the key is to actively discuss and make decisions about the future. I am constantly learning about creative living choices from the people I meet and would like to share an idea or two.

This past winter I worked with two inspiring brothers. They called me suddenly one afternoon. I rushed over to meet them, as they seemed insistent that I should, and I was instantly engaged. I visited them all afternoon, listening, laughing and learning. They were both dads and granddads who were fiercely independent in spite of physical constraints, including the nasty, relentless disease of multiple sclerosis ravaging one brother and spinal injuries plaguing the other. They shared a modest home in which each had one side of the house, with a kitchen in the middle. One brother was a fabulous cook, and I looked forward to the smells of his treats each visit. They were in poor shape physically but, mentally and verbally, they were feisty. I am not sure if they really liked each other from some of the banter back and forth. Talk about the "Odd Couple!" Whatever their relationship really was, it worked. The colorful stories were sometimes a bit more than I was used to hearing. I can't share them here, but I am blushing just thinking of what I heard. I remember that it struck me as I was listening how these brothers supported each other. They were healthy in that they knew they needed each other and had figured out how to make it work. Even though they had children, it didn't seem like the children were in a position to assist them with daily needs. And I am sure they wouldn't ask for help because of their personalities. When I met them, they had a new plan.

They knew that their physical needs were getting more demanding and this arrangement couldn't last forever. One had an ex-wife and daughter in another state who lived in a large home. The other brother said, "Let's move in with your ex-wife because I get along with her just fine!" It seemed perfectly logical as I got to know these two. They brainstormed and came up with a couple of ideas. One was to move into the downstairs of her home, which had a separate entrance. The other thought was to use the proceeds from the sale of both homes and find something that would be even more suitable for the three of them. They could pool their resources, comfortably buy a home together and share expenses. I particularly enjoyed the notion of an ex-husband, ex-wife and brother/ex-brother-in-law living together under one roof. They sold their Missoula home, moved and — as far as I know — they are making their plan work. I sure would like to visit and learn from them some more. They were an inspiration.

Here's another story that I heard recently. Two weeks ago, we packed up Carter (our younger son) from his junior year at college and drove him home from Arizona. One night we stopped at a hot spring for the evening and enjoyed a soak after a day in the car. There I met two sisters, who seemed about my age. They live two hours in opposite directions and had arranged to meet and enjoy the day soaking together. These two women obviously enjoyed each other's company, a little better than those two bantering brothers. As the conversation twisted and turned, we started talking about places to live. Then one sister remarked that she wished she had kept her larger home in a town she loved, so she could have shared it with her sister. She said it was big enough for them each to have their own space and privacy, but they could have enjoyed living in the same town and supporting each other if ever needed. The more we talked, the more excited they became at the prospects and possibilities. We were still talking as I got out of the warm water, dried off and went to find Carter, who had disappeared much earlier as I daydreamed with these sisters. What a warm conversation.

The best inspiration for me and many others is that as we age, there are more options about how we live than we have ever considered in the past. As we continue to have these dialogues with each other, even more ideas will surface. We shouldn't feel bogged down by our homes, their maintenance, and physical constraints. The important thing is to figure out how to spend more time soaking in the springs, connecting with your ex or just watching the game, whatever brings you the most satisfaction and the best stories to share.

Cooperative Living—An Attractive Option

While we were preparing for our older son, Leland, to head off to an out-of-state college, I was certainly going through a roller coaster of emotions. Life was changing for all of us as our relationship was evolving into a new arena and finances would be stretched. Leland was determined to help in any way possible. After his first year, immersed in the dorm/freshman experience, he discovered a cooperative living house located just steps from the campus. From then until his graduation, he became an integral member of a very interesting living concept. While I was familiar with co-ops, I learned along with him how they work.

A cooperative housing community is a corporation formed by a group of individuals to own and manage real estate. The owners are on the board and set forth the rules of operation and ownership. Their "stock" in the company is a percentage of the total real property. Members then lease the property, which pays for expenses such as taxes, insurance, loan fees and maintenance costs. What I learned, observing Leland's experience, was how cost effective and enriching the co-op life can be. Each person was required to assume tasks such as cleaning, cooking and administration. Leland's charge was to act as the group mediator, which kept him busy and constantly learning.

I talk with fellow boomers every week who are analyzing their living options and choices. People grapple with the notion of ownership versus renting, Many boomers are used to homeownership and find it hard to completely give up the independence of making their own real estate choices. In Missoula, people are most familiar with the concepts of condominiums and townhomes. Clients whom I work with consider moving into those living environments as a means to share their maintenance needs and costs.

Condominium owners own their living space. They are members of the condominium association and are jointly owners of, and responsible for, the land and the buildings outside their living space. Each condo association can be different, but usually there is an ownership meeting once per year. During the year, the board or a committee often hires a management company to direct the business on a day-to-day basis.

Townhomes can be described as somewhat of a combination of a single-family residence and a condo. Townhome ownership is defined by a legal description of a piece of property on which the residence is built. A group of townhomes built together may also include some properties (open space, for example) owned jointly.

In Missoula, we see condos and townhomes frequently, although sometimes the terms can be confused. But co-ops are a concept that may become more commonplace and can look a little different, depending on how they are developed by the members.

Cooperatives can be created on large properties, where each member lives in their own personal home. The members buy the property jointly, build their own residence and own shares in the co-op proportionate to their investment. In larger cities, co-ops have existed for a long time as a means for people to purchase a large building, manage it themselves and keep costs low in high-rent areas. For boomers in towns like Missoula, it could be an opportunity to move into a home that better suits someone's needs. In tougher financial times, people still need safe, low-maintenance homes. They still want their own home-cooked meals and room for their

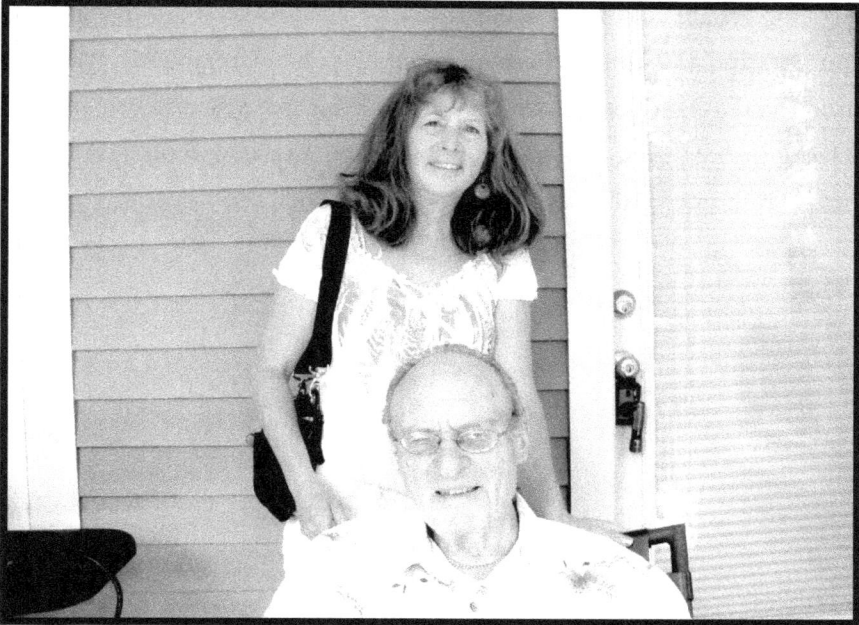

Marshall, Shelley's husband and my brother-in-law, on the deck outside their beautiful one-level condominium.

pets. They want ample space for their families to visit comfortably. But, for example, during a recession when their homes are selling for less than they anticipated, it may not seem possible to have all of these choices.

Co-ops may be a nice option and a possible solution as boomers move into the next phase of their lives. As Leland and we found, the added benefit is the enrichment of life with the other co-op owners. Think about a boomer co-op and the resources that would be there: retired plumbers, artists, actors, social workers, professors, lawyers, nurses and doctors. Not to mention retired architects, builders and city employees who would have the expertise and time to support the co-op. I suppose a mediator and a chef could come in handy as well. It is fun to consider the possibilities.

As boomers are coming of age, I think we need to keep exploring living concepts and adapting them to meet our new and changing lifestyles. We need to take the resources we have, even if they are less, and become creative with them. Co-ops may be the solution as a way to pool our hard-earned resources and knowledge to create an enriched lifestyle.

Cohousing—Another Unique Living Opportunity

Over the years I have written about aging in place, rightsizing, downsizing, making accommodations to existing homes and even moving to different towns. The article that received the most feedback was the one in which I talked about exploring different living options. And the concept that piqued the most interest was about my son's experiences with cooperative living in college. People asked why that can't be an option for the aging population. Of course, it is a viable alternative, as are others, outside of traditional single-family housing. Since that time, I have found out more about how inventive individuals are taking this matter into their own hands. There are more choices and, once again, boomers are forging the way.

One December, I was visiting my family in Boston. My sister's friend Peg graciously offered my niece Rachel a place to stay, as space was filling up where we were sleeping. Her home was within walking distance, so we accompanied Rachel to Peg's home in Cambridge one evening. As we entered her courtyard, I was drawn in immediately. There were gardens and sculptures and lovely seating arrangements. Inside was a warm, inviting living room with a piano and other spaces that I could see around the corner. This felt like someplace I may have been before, but I knew I hadn't. I soon learned that I had entered a cohousing neighborhood.

Peg welcomed us to her home, a private apartment in the building. My sister laughed and smiled, as I started asking a string of questions about this place. She knows me well and settled in for a visit filled with lively discussions about alternative living choices. It was obvious that Peg, a night person like me, truly enjoyed talking about her home and community. She was one of the original organizers. I was excited to hear her story. She had sold her home when newly single in the '90s and was trying to decide what would be her next move. She met other people in similar situations. They pooled their money and resources from the sales of their homes and found not only the perfect housing solution, but also a rich lifestyle. I learned cohousing emerged in Denmark over 30 years ago and the first in the U.S. was completed in 1991. Many are intergenerational, while some are designed specifically for seniors. The common thread is that they are designed to encourage social interaction while still maintaining individual living spaces and autonomy. There is some great information on the website: *http://www.cambridgecohousing.org/index.html*

I particularly enjoyed a 1998 New Year's card that someone posted on the website. It describes the lifestyle at the building, which includes a community of 90 members living in 41 units. The homes are townhouses, individual homes and apartment-sized units. In addition, residents cooperatively enjoy the use of community spaces including a dining room, library, workshop, laundry and outdoor gardens. It was evident from this letter that the members are active both politically and recreationally in the larger metropolitan area. By sharing day-to-day maintenance and daily chores, they find more time to contribute to their larger community and have more time for fun activities.

I feel enriched learning about cohousing. Once more, I learned that there are many ways to live, depending on our needs and resources. It's opened up another perspective of how many choices there are if we continue to explore housing opportunities.

Afterward

Over fifteen years have passed since I first called Sherry Devlin, editor of the *Missoulian*, offering to write a real estate article. During those years, I have worked full time as a broker/owner of my own real estate company in Missoula, and, to my good fortune, my son Leland decided to join me.

I now own a historic building downtown from where I run the business. My desk faces the big windows that look out to the covered front porch with its highbacked rocking chairs, Broadway Street, the local theater company and our brand new public library.

There are no parking meters outside, which was one of my requirements when we were searching for a space. Clients can park out front, read our historic plaque on the way in, and talk real estate.

In the bookshelf behind my desk, I keep a flyer I compiled that lists some of my articles from the *Missoulian*. When certain topics come up in client meetings, as they often do, I pull out that list and point to an article that's applicable. I usually paraphrase the contents; I tell the goofy story, and we go on with our work.

When people are in the midst of their real estate transactions, they find it more stressful and complicated than they thought it would be. One client said at the end, "Joy, you said this would be hard, but it was wickedly hard."

I changed the names and some of the details to avoid uncomfortable interactions in our small-ish town. Inevitably—at the post office or the farmer's market or somewhere else about town—I'd see a familiar face and remember afterward that they were the "inspiration" for an article. Sometimes, these stories were the result of a deep frustration with someone, and, frankly, they provided a great outlet for me. Others were fun memories as I enjoyed a laugh at my younger self.

I also found that it didn't matter when an article was written: during a recession, a buyer's market, a seller's market, in spring or fall, or ten years ago. The messages in these stories still ring true. The common theme is that real estate is much more than buying or selling. It's a process, often during one of life's transitions, that is best to share with someone who will take you along with their experience as a guide.

Of course, the same is true of all professions. Compiling this book was a new experience for me that I couldn't have done without the guidance of Clare Wood, my editor. Her calm, straightforward, quiet support once again taught me to find someone with experience to guide me through a stressful, hard process.

About the Author

Joy Shulman Earls started writing real estate articles for the *Missoulian* while working as a real estate broker in Western Montana. She was also featured in *Montana 55*.

Joy has a Bachelor of Science degree from the University of Michigan and a Master's of Public Administration from University of Montana. As a resident of Missoula for the past 42-plus years, Joy has been human resources director for the city of Missoula and Partners in Home Care, and executive director of the Montana Association of Home Health Agencies. Her work in corporate mediation and facilitation spanned several decades. Some of the most interesting work experiences she had were in the gold mines of Colorado and oil fields of North Dakota.

She is the broker/owner of Joy Earls Real Estate in Missoula. Joy and her husband, Mark, own and operate Earls Construction Inc. Among other projects, they planned, developed, built, and marketed a development for people 55 and older.

She has served on various boards in leadership roles including: the Montana Mediation Association, Montana Association of Registered Land Surveyors, Montana and Missoula chapters of the Society for Human Resource Management, and the Community Dispute Resolution Center of Missoula.

www.ingramcontent.com/pod-product-compliance
Lightning Source LLC
Chambersburg PA
CBHW030529210326
41597CB00013B/1083